LOVING

Virtue and

THE

Happiness in

FINE

Aristotle's *Ethics*

ANNA LÄNNSTRÖM

University of Notre Dame Press

Notre Dame, Indiana

A record of the Library of Congress Cataloging in-Publication Data is available
upon request from the Library of Congress.

⊖ This book is printed on acid-free paper.

to my dad

c o n t e n t s

preface

Is it possible to prove that it is irrational to be unethical? Can we develop an argument that would convince a rational bad man that he should care about ethics? Scholars and laypeople have hoped so, and in recent years some scholars have argued that Aristotle provides such an argument, which goes something like this: We cannot be happy without being ethical; beings like us want to be happy; therefore, it is in our own interest to be ethical, and to neglect ethics is irrational. This argument, then, should persuade any rational man to become ethical. This book argues that Aristotle certainly maintains that we must be ethical in order to be happy and that human nature determines what can count as happiness for us. However, it argues, Aristotle denied that this argument would convince bad men, he believed that such failure of this and other arguments was unavoidable, and he was right in this belief.

The book engages directly with Aristotle's own writings, focusing upon the *Nicomachean Ethics*, and generally relegates discussions with other interpreters to the endnotes.

My interpretation of Aristotle's ethics is indebted to and inspired by a number of scholars, most importantly John McDowell, Martha Nussbaum, Nancy Sherman, and Bernard Williams, and I think their influence is visible throughout. Perhaps my greatest debt is to two articles by John McDowell (1995a and 1995b) because they helped convince me of my second thesis, namely, that Aristotle recognizes that he has no argument that would persuade all rational listeners that ethics is an integral part of the good life. McDowell supports this thesis by arguing that if Aristotle had thought he had such an argument, he would not have limited the audience of the *Ethics* in the way he does. Rather, according to McDowell, Aristotle would have insisted that his audience should include all rational beings, not just those who have been properly educated. I adopt McDowell's argument and I use it as part of my broader argument. Perhaps most importantly, I show that given Aristotle's view of the role of desire in decision making and in habituation, he simply has to deny that arguments can make people ethical.

A number of friends and colleagues, including Klaus Brinkmann, Matthew Caswell, Colin Heydt, Stefan Kalt, Lydia Moland, Leroy Rouner, and David Wong have patiently read the manuscript in various incarnations. Their criticism has always been both encouraging and constructive, and they have helped me immensely. Jeff Gainey's support and enthusiasm was invaluable throughout the revision process. Further, I have especially benefited from the suggestions and criticisms offered by David Roochnik and two anonymous readers at the University of Notre Dame Press. All three helped me to sharpen the focus of the book and to develop the overall argument. Most of all, I am deeply grateful for Leroy Rouner's mentoring and friendship; he has helped me grow as a scholar and as a person.

Barbara Hanrahan, Charles van Hof, Rebecca DeBoer, and the rest of the staff at the University of Notre Dame Press have been a pleasure to work with. I also owe many thanks to Margaret Hyre for her meticulous copy editing and attention to detail.

I am grateful to Stonehill College for giving me a reduced teaching load during the Fall of 2003 when I was finishing the book and to Celia Tam at Boston University's Institute for Philosophy and Religion and Megan Guiney at Stonehill College for providing me with superb and much-needed secretarial assistance as I was revising this manuscript.

abbreviations

References to works by Aristotle use the standard Bekker pagination. Titles of works by Aristotle are abbreviated as follows:

DA	*De Anima*
EE	*Eudemian Ethics*
Met.	*Metaphysics*
NE	*Nicomachean Ethics*
Pol.	*Politics*
Rhet.	*Rhetoric*

Translations I have used are listed in the Works Cited. Unless otherwise noted, quotations from the *Nicomachean Ethics* use Irwin's translations and quotations from the *Politics* use Lord's. In quotations from Irwin's translation, I have replaced "prudence" with "phronêsis" and "prudent," "prudent person," and similar expressions with "phronimos." References throughout the text that are not otherwise identified are to the *Nicomachean Ethics*.

Page references to works by Kant use the standard German edition of Kant's works: *Kant's Gesammelte Schriften*, edited by the Royal Preussian (later German) Academy of Sciences (Berlin: George Reimer, later Walter de Gruyter & Co., 1900–). Titles of his works are abbreviated as follows:

CPrR	*Critique of Practical Reason*
CPR	*Critique of Pure Reason*

G   *Groundwork of the Metaphysics of Morals*
MM   *Metaphysics of Morals*
Religion   *Religion within the Boundaries of Mere Reason*

The English translations of Kant's works that I have used are listed in the Works Cited.

INTRODUCTION

Do bad people reason badly? Many philosophers have answered yes, beginning with Socrates in such dialogues as the *Republic* and the *Gorgias*, where he confronts speakers who deny that ethics provides any genuine reasons for acting. They recognize that acting justly might be useful in many situations, for example, by giving me a good reputation. But why act justly when nobody is watching? Why should I care about doing the "right" or "ethical" thing when it conflicts with what I want? Why not simply dismiss those bothersome, inconvenient notions of duties that I should perform, character traits I should develop, and so on, the better to focus my attention and energies on promoting my own interests? In Book 1 of the *Republic*, Thrasymachus argues that "injustice, when it comes into being on a sufficient scale, is mightier, freer, and more masterful than justice" (344c). In Book 2, Glaucon continues Thrasymachus's argument and asks Socrates to show that justice itself is worth having even if it is accompanied with a reputation for injustice.

Glaucon and Thrasymachus bring challenges from different viewpoints. Thrasymachus denies altogether that ethics provides compelling reasons for action, while Glaucon is a well brought up young man who believes that ethics matters, but who nevertheless seeks a justification for his view, a rational account of why he should be ethical even in situations where it would put him at a great disadvantage. I will refer to someone like Glaucon as a *skeptic*. A skeptic, in my usage here, is a person who feels as though ethics has a legitimate role but who is not *rationally* convinced of that and who wants to bracket that feeling and be convinced by arguments with "neutral" premises. I will refer to somebody like Thrasymachus as a *bad* person, in my definition a seemingly rational person who stands outside ethics.

In the *Republic*, Socrates accepts Glaucon's challenge and tries to show that virtue in itself is worth having. Without it, he concludes, our souls will be unbalanced and sick. How then could it not be profitable to be just? Glaucon agrees and says that the inquiry has "become ridiculous by now" (445a). If life with a corrupted body does not seem worth living, surely, he argues, life with a corrupt soul is even less so.

While Socrates convinces Glaucon, Thrasymachus fades from the conversation, showing no signs of being persuaded, which suggests that Plato did not believe that Socrates' argument would persuade bad men. Most readers, too, bad and decent alike, remain unpersuaded by his argument. Still, we are likely to think that Socrates was right in trying to convince Glaucon and Thrasymachus and that their questions require answers in the form of an argument that should convince them and every other rational person that ethics matters. That argument would meet Glaucon's challenge, showing that it is in my interest to be just even if my justice will be accompanied with every appearance of injustice and that ethics provides good reasons for acting justly even when it requires us to act in ways that seem to be useless or even dangerous.

But in order to avoid circularity, our argument needs to start outside ethics, providing an answer to the bad man's challenge based upon premises that he would accept. If we cannot answer Thrasymachus, it seems that we have to admit that we have no good reason for condemning his behavior— we just do not like it. In addition, our own ethical convictions may suddenly seem unjustified and arbitrary. Perhaps we act ethically (or at least we try to) simply because that was how we were raised. We believe that this is how we should act because that is what our parents told us when we were children. But then, if that is all we have, we do not know that what we were taught is right and true, that we were not just "brainwashed." In short, if we cannot provide an extra-ethical grounding for ethics, ethics might seem to hang unsupported in the air, liable to collapse and fall.

The resurgence of interest in Aristotle during the past few decades appears to have been at least in part a response to this perceived need for a grounding. The Aristotelian (re)turn was initiated by Elizabeth Anscombe's "Modern Moral Philosophy" (1958). She was disappointed with utilitarianism and deontology, arguing that they were unable to give their ethical rules normative force without a divine lawgiver.[1] Anscombe suggested that Aristotle might provide a naturalistic grounding for ethics.[2] Other writers agreed and added that Aristotle's writings also seemed to include important and plausible insights about the nature of ethics and human beings that utilitarianism and deontology often have neglected. For example, he insisted that we cannot expect exactness in ethics, he focused upon virtues and character, he showed great sensitivity to the issue of moral luck, and he gave the desiring part of the soul a crucial part in decision making.

When I began this project, I shared the hope of other neo-Aristotelians that Aristotle might provide a solid grounding for ethics in the sense that he would provide a defense of ethics that would at least in principle convince people like Glaucon and Thrasymachus. I believed that Aristotle provided an argument to ethics from human nature or happiness (*eudaimonia*), which can be summarized as follows: He starts with a pool of facts about human nature, including information about our characteristic activity (*ergon*) as rational agents. Then, he examines these facts about us, asking what a good life would be for such beings and developing a notion of the happy life, the life that should serve as our end (*telos*). With that notion of the happy life in hand, he argues that the virtues are the qualities that promote our happiness. They are necessary conditions; we cannot be happy without being good. Beings like us want to be happy so we have to be good. And then, it seems, we simply need to study ourselves and discover that link between virtue and happiness to see that ethics provides genuine reasons for human action. We have an argument for ethics that does not simply presuppose the views of decent people about what one ought to do but which starts from metaphysical or psychological facts about human beings, facts that are accessible to all rational human beings. We should be ethical because being ethical is a necessary part of happiness. Thus, we know why ethics provides genuine reasons for action—it promotes an end which we all pursue and it is necessary for the attainment of that end. Consequently, Aristotle's argument should convince bad men and skeptics alike—as long as they are rational.

In the past, something like this has been a common reading of Aristotle. In W.D. Ross's view, for instance, Aristotle views actions as morally right if and only if they bring us closer to the human good.[3] Similarly, Frederick Copleston argues that Aristotle uses natural human tendencies to ground ethics, although he does not believe that Aristotle is fully successful.[4] More recently, Bernard Williams gives a reading along these lines. He argues that Aristotle's project is to try to "ground ethical life in well-being, [and that he] sought determinate conclusions about the shape of a whole life, from substantive beliefs about human nature" (1985, 54).[5] Similarly, Terence Irwin argues that Aristotle derives his account of the virtues from the human essence, more precisely, from the fact that we are rational agents (1989).[6] Once we understand what it means to be a human being, then, we can show what the good life is for such a being, and we can show any rational human agent that the virtues play a crucial role in that life. This gives a reason to act ethically that should persuade all rational human beings; if they do not act ethically, they will not be able to live the good life that they want to live.

Other scholars have been more skeptical about Aristotle's ability to disprove Thrasymachus. Martha Nussbaum and Julia Annas agree that Aristotle argues to ethics from facts about human beings, but both note that the facts in question are not value-neutral but rather (something like) facts about what is important to human beings about human nature.[7] This suggests that whatever argument we came up with may not persuade our interlocutors because they will quite reasonably reply that our argument begs the question. Others have suggested that Aristotle is neither able nor willing to give us the argument that we want. Richard Kraut, for example, argues that Aristotle does not in fact derive the human good from human nature. Rather, he suggests, Aristotle believes that our view of the human good determines our view of human nature.[8] Consequently, neither Aristotle nor we can use human nature to persuade those who disagree with us about the human end; they will not accept our view of human nature either. Similarly, Peter Simpson denies that Aristotle explains virtues based on *eudaimonia*. Rather, he argues, virtue is the prior notion and *eudaimonia* is defined in terms of virtue.[9] Finally, John McDowell has repeatedly attacked both the quest for foundations in ethics and the attempt to use Aristotle to provide such foundations. He argues that Aristotle simply is not interested in proving to Thrasymachus or any other bad man that Aristotle is right and they wrong, and he suggests that we would do well by following Aristotle here.[10]

I share the skepticism of these latter thinkers and will argue that Aristotle is both unable and unwilling to provide the argument we seek. My discussion is based primarily on the *Nicomachean Ethics*, drawing occasionally on other works, especially the *Politics*.[11] I will examine Aristotle's view of moral education and of the interplay between desire and reason, showing that if Aristotle's view is correct, as I think it is, it will be impossible to provide such arguments. We cannot disprove the bad man in terms that he would accept and consequently we cannot provide the sort of extra-ethical grounding for ethics that many of us hope for. In addition, I will argue, Aristotle recognized it was impossible.

In the first chapter, I begin by considering the respective roles of reason and desire in Aristotelian goodness and moral education. For Aristotle, being good involves making good decisions, and such decisions in turn have a conative as well as a rational component; you cannot make good decisions without having both right desire and right reason, without loving the fine (*kalon*) and being able to figure out what the fine requires. Proper desire thus plays a crucial role in our ethical lives as an essential part of good character and of correct ethical motivation. (If I do not want to act generously, I am not generous.) Goodness also requires virtue of character, which we acquire through habituation. Because we become virtuous through habituation, it is tempting to view virtue as an unthinking matter of having the right desires and habits. However, I will argue that this cannot be so; virtue is a habit, but a *choosing* habit (*hexis prohairetikê*) and therefore must have a significant rational component. Like decision making, virtue requires both reason and desire. Indeed, I will argue, full virtue requires more than being able to figure out what to do; it also requires understanding why we should do it. This may seem to require the ability to provide an argument that could persuade the bad man, but I will try to show that it does not.

To underscore the significance of Aristotle's view that desire has a key role in virtue and decision making, it is helpful to contrast it with Kant's equally important but radically different view. In the second chapter, I consider their fundamental disagreement concerning the proper role of desires and inclinations in moral action. I argue against Kant's view that morality requires motivation for action that is independent of our inclinations. I suggest that Aristotle is right in saying that inclinations have moral significance and that they can and must be part of moral motivation, thus insisting on an empirical account of moral motivation. However, I argue that if we follow Aristotle rather than Kant on this point, we have to pay a steep price. That is, we must face Kant's famous objection to empiricist ethics in general. Kant argues that empiricism cannot explain the nature of moral obligation. To put it differently, it can justify hypothetical but not categorical imperatives. Aristotle might be able to justify saying "if you want to be happy, be moral" but he cannot explain why we must obey the categorical command to be moral.

If ethics binds only through such hypothetical imperatives, it ceases to be the highest end and becomes a means to that end. It might then be rendered unnecessary by somebody who finds a different means to the end. In the third chapter I take up Book 10 of the *Ethics*, where exactly this seems to happen. There, Aristotle notes that there are two candidates for *eudaimonia*—a life of character virtue and a life of theoretical virtue (*theôria*)—and he argues that *theôria* is higher. This suggests that those who excel at *theôria* can neglect ethics and still attain *eudaimonia*. They do not violate the Aristotelian hypothetical imperative because they have found a different route to happiness. I will argue that the Kantian challenge is irresistible on this point. Aristotle fails to show that it would be impossible to reach *eudaimonia* by focusing upon *theôria* at the expense of ethics. From within ethics, we can see that an unethical theoretician would be missing something crucial, but he would not be able to see it (unless he were rehabituated), even though he is supremely rational. Ethics thus seems to become optional for him.

Now, it may not matter much that the theoretician can bypass ethics. After all, such people are rare. Aristotle could accept that the unethical theoretician might be happy but argue that because most people are not capable of living a life of *theôria*, they must be ethical in order to have a chance to be happy. So what argument could Aristotle provide for the rest of us, including skeptics and bad people? Can he persuade us that happiness requires virtue? In the fourth chapter, I suggest that Aristotle does indeed present an argument concerning the role of ethics in the good life which starts in the very beginning of the *Ethics* with an analysis of the teleological structure of human action and the introduction of a hierarchy of ends. I outline and evaluate the argument. However, while I defend his argument as plausible and powerful, I suggest that it will fail to persuade the bad person that ethics has intrinsic and not just instrumental value. It does not prove that we must embrace the human end as our end and it does not show that the ethical virtues have intrinsic value. Consequently, it will not persuade the bad man that he must change if he is to live well.

But perhaps the Book 1 argument is not the only option. Might Aristotle have or provide materials for other arguments that would defend ethics based upon human nature or *eudaimonia*? The good man knows why he should be good; does not that mean that he has access to an argument that would do the job? The final chapter explores the failure of several possible arguments to ethics from human nature and from *eudaimonia*, and I conclude that we cannot present an argument from either of these two starting points which would persuade the bad man. The basic problem is that our argument will have to begin from a starting point (*archê*) which we acquire through proper habituation and which the bad man does not share (and which the skeptic brackets).

I argue that Aristotle recognized this problem and consequently did not try to develop such an argument. Following McDowell, I argue that if Aristotle had believed that he had such an argument, he would have indicated that all rational human beings could benefit from hearing it (1995a and 1995b). He does not do so but instead repeatedly argues that the hearers must be rightly educated. Furthermore, as Simpson points out, trying to derive virtue from *eudaimonia* gets Aristotle backwards because Aristotle views virtue and not *eudaimonia* as the prior notion (1992). Thus, Aristotle agrees with Kant that it is wrongheaded to present arguments for ethics which assume that ethics is a means to some further end. Although Aristotle certainly believes and argues that we must be good in order to be happy and that human nature determines what can count as a good life for us, he did not believe that this could be proven to those who did not already believe it. Thus, he rejects the Socratic conversation with skeptics and bad men as pointless.[12] Because of the relationship between reason and desire, no argument for ethics would convince a bad man. Consequently, we have to view our failure to convince Thrasymachus as unavoidable. It is impossible to meet his demand for extra-ethical reasons in favor of always being ethical because there are no such reasons. In fact, I will argue, as soon as we think it makes sense to ask for such reasons, we have reduced ethics to the status of a means, which it is not, and will then find that it is an inefficient and sometimes unnecessary means; acting ethically may not make us happy at all and we can be happy without it.

The impossibility of an argument for ethics that would persuade all rational beings that they should be ethical does not make conversations about ethical matters superfluous. It does mean, however, that the list of possible participants must be limited to those who already love the fine and who have their desires under some sort of control. I argue that the *Ethics* is written for that sort of audience, aiming to help them improve their self-understanding and encouraging them to become better human beings. Arguments alone cannot make them good, but if the desire is there, arguments can help make them better. Yet the failure of our conversations with Thrasymachus has disturbing implications for our ability to reach rational agreement even with other good people. This is a problem that Aristotle does not seem to recognize, but which we must face.

chapter one

BEING AND
BECOMING GOOD

What is involved in being and becoming good? Do good people know something that bad people do not? This chapter examines Aristotle's view of the interplay of reason and desire in human goodness and moral education. To identify the good man, Aristotle argues, we need to consider his decisions (*prohaireseis*) because they both express and shape his character; courageous people make courageous decisions and they become courageous by consistently deciding to act courageously.[1] A good man makes good decisions whereas a bad man does not. Good decision making requires practical wisdom (*phronêsis*). However, good decisions also have a significant conative component and thus in addition require virtue of character as well as a love of the fine (*kalon*). Being and becoming good is a combination of good reason and good desire. The good person must know what to do and why it should be done, and his desires must be well habituated.

After a preliminary discussion of the rational and conative aspects of decision making, I will deal with the role of the fine in decision making and with our desire for the fine and its role as *telos* and motivation in the good life. I will also explain what it means to say that the good person loves the fine and show why such love is crucial in Aristotle's understanding of the good person. Finally, I will discuss virtue of character, focusing upon Aristotle's definition of virtue as a *hexis prohairetikê*, a "choosing disposition/habit," and his view that virtue is acquired through habituation. I consider what it means to say that virtue is a *hexis*, asking whether it suggests that virtue and

9

habituation are largely unthinking matters and that the intellect has little role to play in the virtuous life. I argue that this cannot be so because virtue is not just a *hexis* but a *hexis prohairetikê*, not just a habit but a choosing habit. Thus, it requires good reasoning. I therefore suggest that habituation and teaching must be intertwined and stress that true goodness for Aristotle requires significant thought based upon correct desires. Indeed, I will argue that the intellectual component is not restricted to the need to know what to do; true virtue also requires a grasp of the reasons for why that is so. The good person knows why she should act rightly. This "why" promises a possible argument which we could use to persuade the bad man that he should be good, but I will argue in later chapters that this promise is illusory.

DECISION MAKING

Aristotle argues that in order to make a decision (*prohairesis*) at all, we need both desire and reason:

> Thought by itself moves nothing; what moves us is goal-directed thought concerned with action [and] . . . acting well is the goal and desire is for the goal. That is why decision is either understanding combined with desire or desire combined with thought, and this is the sort of principle that a human being is. (1139b1–5)

Decision is understanding with desire, desire with thought. Desire is necessary in order for us to move at all. If we did not want anything, we would do nothing. To put the point differently, our movement is teleological. When we move, we aim at a goal, something that we want. Such movement might be merely instinctual. If so, it has no cognitive component and does not involve decision. It is a mere movement and not an action (*praxis*). Unlike mere movement, an action in the strict sense involves both reason and desire. Aristotle expresses the rational aspect of decision making by saying that decision requires deliberation. Generally, Aristotle writes, "what is decided is what has been previously deliberated. For decision involves reason and thought" (1112a15).[2]

My decisions must be good if I am to live well. As Aristotle puts it, "the reason must be true and the desire correct" (1139a25). In other words, I must want the right good and know how to get there: "There are two things that [living] well consists in for all: one of these is in the correct positing of the aim and end of actions; the other, discovering the actions that bear on the end . . . [S]ometimes the aim is finely posited but in acting they miss achieving it, and sometimes they achieve everything with a view to the end, but the end they posited was bad. And sometimes they miss both" (*Pol.* 1331b26–33). I may fail to live well through a failure of reason. That is, I might not be able to figure out how to reach my chosen ends.[3] But I might also live poorly if my desires are inappropriate. If I do not desire a good end, I will not live well even if I correctly determine the means to my chosen end.[4] If I do not reason well, I must learn to reason better. If I do not desire the right end, my desires must improve.

Aristotle argues that correct desire includes a desire for the fine (*kalon*). Unless I love the fine, then, I will not be able to make good decisions or to live well. The fine expresses both what I should do and the motivation of the good person. Thus, to say that an act is fine is to say it is the right thing to do, and that a good person would therefore want to do it. Before examining this view further, we need to discuss the term *kalon* and its translation.

Kalon

The basic sense of *kalon* is "beautiful," but from Homer onward the term *kalon* has also been used in an ethical sense, which is how it is used in Aristotle's ethical treatises. The question of how to translate this usage of *kalon* in Aristotle (and elsewhere) is notoriously difficult. Joseph Owens reviews an extensive list of possible translations, including "the morally good," "beautiful," "noble," "fine," "honorable," "seemly," and "right" (1981). It seems to me that an ideal translation of *kalon* would fulfill the following requirements: First, it would indicate that saying that an action is *kalon* is to say that it is the right thing to do. Second, it would suggest that saying that an action is *kalon* provides a motive for the well-habituated person. Third, because *kalon* can be used to say that something is beautiful, the translation would have an aesthetic dimension. Fourth, our translation would not tempt us to import foreign philosophical ideas, and it would fit well into an Aristotelian framework. Finally, because familiar translations are less distracting than new ones, they are preferable unless the new translation is clearly better.

Finding a translation that fulfills all these requirements seems impossible. I have chosen to use "fine" because I find it better than the alternatives.[5] I agree with Owens that this use of "fine" is a bit "elevated" and "stilted" and that it fails to capture the obligatory force of *kalon*. The latter problem is a serious limitation and, if there were no other considerations, I would prefer "right" or "seemly," which stress this aspect of *kalon*. As Owens points out, "seemly," also has the added advantage of emphasizing "moderation and measure" (1981, 32–33). In my view, though, these choices have more serious limitations than does "fine." "Right" has such strong associations with rules and legal rights and with a variety of rights-based ethical theories that I consider it an unacceptable choice within an Aristotelian context.[6] Furthermore, because I will be discussing the obligatory and motivating force of *kalon* throughout, we will constantly be reminded of these aspects, so I find it less important to use a word that stresses them. I choose "fine" over "seemly" for three reasons: it is more commonly used in the secondary literature; what is "seemly" seems to be relative to each culture, but what is *kalon* is not supposed to be; and "fine" captures the double meaning of *kalon*: beautiful and morally good.[7] Finally, I find its very elevation and stiltedness useful because it prevents us from assuming that we know exactly what Aristotle means by it. It suggests that he is talking about something that we must work to become familiar with and that is exactly the impression I want it to convey.

Acting for the Sake of the Fine

Aristotle's discussion of individual virtues and virtuous persons repeatedly expresses the motivation of the virtuous person in terms of the fine. Consider for example the following passages:

> The brave person, then, aims at the fine [*kalou dê heneka*] when he stands firm and acts in accord with bravery. (1115b23–24)

> Actions in accord with virtues are fine and aim at the fine [*tou kalou heneka*]. (1120a24)

> [Wasteful people] care nothing for the fine [*to mêden tou kalou phrontizein*], and so take from any source without scruple. . . . This is why their ways of giving are not generous either, since they are not fine, do not aim at the fine, and are not done in the right way [*ou gar kalai, oude toutou heneka, oude ôs dei*] (1121b1–5).[8]

Doing what courage requires is thus a special case of doing what the fine requires. In order for somebody's character to be virtuous, it is not enough that he does the fine thing; he must be doing it for the sake of the fine. To be virtuous is to be motivated by the fine. Aristotle's references to "aiming at the fine" serve as a shorthand for all virtuous motivation. When somebody acts courageously, I can say that she is motivated by the fine or I can be more specific and say that she is motivated by courage.[9]

Aristotle notes that human beings have three objects of choice—the pleasant, the expedient (*sumpherontos*), and the fine—and three corresponding objects of aversion (1104b31). All our decisions and actions aim at (at least) one of the three objects of choice (or at avoiding one of the objects of aversion). Young children are simply motivated by pleasure and pain.[10] Indeed, Aristotle explains that the pleasant never releases its grip. Pleasure "is implied by every object of choice, since what is fine and what is expedient appears pleasant as well" (1105a1–2). Therefore, Aristotle argues that to become good requires learning to "find enjoyment or pain in the right things" (1104b10). As we grow older and begin to reason, we start to deliberate concerning what is advantageous to ourselves, and the expedient becomes one of our motivations. If all goes well, we also learn to recognize that the fine is an object of choice and that we ought to pursue it.

Before we become good, the three objects of choice are often at odds, pulling us in different and opposing directions. Once we view the fine as a motive in its own right, our understanding of what is truly advantageous and pleasant should start to shift, so that "doing the fine" will seem more advantageous and more pleasant than not doing it, which will strike us as neither pleasant nor advantageous. The good person does what he ought to do because it is the right thing to do. However, because of the aforementioned shift, he will still be doing what is beneficial to him; a person with practical wisdom is "able to deliberate finely about things that are good and beneficial [*sumpheronta*] for himself, not about some restricted area . . . but about what sorts of things promote living well in general" (1140a26–29). And finally, he does what is pleasant because doing the fine is pleasant to him. Thus for a good person, the three are in unison. That is, he recognizes the fine as the most pleasant and most advantageous. Consequently, I do not view the three motivations as "irreducibly distinct" as Burnyeat does (1980, 87). On the contrary, a central goal of Aristotelian moral education is to make the three merge. McDowell expresses the dominance of the fine by saying that it will "silence" all other considerations, not just override them (1980, 370). I would prefer to say that it "incorporates and transforms" all other considerations. "Silencing" suggests that we would no longer care about what is beneficial or pleasant, or that the three motives conflict in such a way that we can act on only one of them. Neither conclusion is true, though in some cases "silencing" is an appropriate description. Aristotle acknowledges that in some situations (for instance, dying in battle) doing the fine will not be pleasant even to the temperate man. In such situations, the fine will be what matters for the good man, and we might say that it silences all other considerations.

Developing harmony among our three motives will take time and effort and very few people, if any, get that far. The vast majority will become not temperate but, at best, continent. Both the continent and the temperate person regard the fine as an independent motive for action (not just as a means to the other two). They would not pursue something pleasant if that meant doing something shameful. However, while the continent person has understood that the fine should be his highest motive, he does not experience it as more advantageous and pleasant than its alternatives. He knows that the fine should silence other considerations, but as yet it does not. Consequently, he has to struggle to make the fine override other considerations. The temperate person no longer views that formerly pleasant thing as pleasant and thus it does not even pose a temptation.[11]

While the continent person is inferior to the temperate person, he is vastly superior to those who do not act in any way for the sake of the fine. Such people may well do what is fine, but they are not motivated by it. They may for example be motivated by knowing that they will be honored for doing the fine thing and punished for not doing it, and thus pursue the fine as a means to public honor. Aristotle suggests that this is the best we can expect from the many. They are not able to refrain from actions because those actions are base, but rather only if they know they will be punished. That is, their decisions are not made based upon an understanding of the fine:

> The many naturally obey fear, not shame; they avoid what is base because of the penalties, not because it is disgraceful. For since they live by their feelings, they pursue their proper pleasures and the sources of them, and avoid the opposed pains, and have not even a notion of what is fine and [hence] truly pleasant, since they have had no taste of it. (1179b11–16)

They refrain from following their desires only when external control is imposed.

If we act like the many, Aristotle argues, we are (at best) acting virtuously without being virtuous. We do the right things but not for the right reasons. This point emerges strongly in Aristotle's discussion of courage. He lists several states that resemble courage without really being courage. While the people in such states do what they ought to do, they do not do it for the right reasons. The so-called courage of citizens is not really courage because while citizens with such "courage" stand firm against dangers, as they should, they do not do so for the sake of the fine but "with the aim of avoiding reproaches and legal penalties and of winning honors" (1116a20). One may also stand firm due to compulsion or anger. In contrast, Aristotle stresses, "brave people act because of the fine" (1116b32). Similarly, Aristotle chastises the vulgar person because he "aims not at the fine but at the display of his wealth" (1123a25). Such people are doing the right thing but for the wrong reasons. They fail to recognize that the *kalon* must be pursued for its own sake; they do not see that it is an intrinsic end. Or, what comes down to the same thing, the *kalon* is not yet an object of choice for them (or it is at least not the dominant one).[12]

In contrast, the temperate, the continent, and the incontinent person all know that the fine is imposing a necessity upon them; they would be wrong if they were to neglect it. It is right to do the fine and it would be wrong to choose not to do it. This obligatory nature of the fine is suggested by Aristotle's use of *kalon* interchangeably with *dei* (one should/ought) in the *Ethics*. Consider for instance the following passages:

> Pleasure causes us to do base actions, and pain causes us to abstain from fine ones. That is why we need to have had the appropriate upbringing . . . to make us find enjoyment or pain in the right things [*hois dei*]. (1104b10–12)

> Fear of some bad things . . . is actually right [*dei*] and fine. (1115a12)

> The generous person will also aim at the fine in his giving, and will give correctly [*orthôs*]; for he will give to the right people, the right amounts, at the right time [*hois gar dei kai hosa kai hote*]. (1120a24–26)

> If someone gives to the wrong people [*ou dei*] or does not aim at the fine, but gives for some other reason, he will not be called generous. (1120a28–29)[13]

In this emphasis on right and wrong and on what one should and should not do, we come close to our own understanding of ethical motivation. I agree with Annas and Korsgaard that the requirements of the fine generally express ethical requirements.[14] When Aristotle writes that we should act for the sake of the fine, he is requiring us to do *x* because it is right and not just because it is pleasant or expedient. However, acting for the sake of the fine is a notion broader than "acting for the sake of ethics" and broader, especially, than "acting for the sake of morality."[15] As Sherman and Nussbaum both note, Aristotle generally draws no sharp distinction between ethical and non-ethical considerations.[16] Indeed, the fine seems to include everything that we might say would be covered by a sense of noblesse oblige. It includes what the gentleman ought to do, or what civility requires.[17] That is, it includes ethics, but it also addresses what we today would consider to be questions of manners, style, and politeness. For example, the fine makes demands about how to dress (not too gaudy). However, it seems to me that when Aristotle talks throughout the *Ethics* and the *Politics* about the right thing to do (*to deon*), about the fine, and about the sort of people we should try to become, he is usually speaking about recognizably ethical matters.[18] Furthermore, while he lists wit as a virtue together with justice, courage, generosity, and temperance, among others, he seems to regard wit as much less important because he spends much more time discussing the others, and because he describes people who do not recognize the force of the fine as intemperate and unjust, not as boorish (lacking wit). Finally, in certain cases, Aristotle does seem to give ethical considerations absolute priority, suggesting that there are some things one should never do (slay one's father), no matter what the consequences of refusing would be. Thus, certain ethical principles outweigh all other possible considerations; they are preemptive and supreme. We are justified then, in thinking that when Aristotle talks about the fine, he is talking about something like ethics as we understand it; but we must remember that he is talking not only about ethics but also about living well in other respects.

Loving the Fine: Making Good Decisions

We have seen that Aristotle denies that decision is a purely rational matter. Again, Aristotle writes that "decision is either understanding combined with desire [*orektikos nous*] or desire combined with thought [*orexis dianoêtikê*]" (1139b5). To indicate the crucial role of desire here, I often use the phrase "loving the fine" instead of "acting for the sake of the fine."[19] The phrase occurs a few times in the *Ethics*, for example in 1.8 where Aristotle writes: "The things that please lovers of the fine [*philokalois*] are things pleasant by nature. Actions in accord with virtue are pleasant by nature, so that they both please lovers of the fine and are pleasant in their own right" (1099a13–15).[20]

Aristotle's distinction between the temperate and the continent persons illuminates the importance of proper desires. While both do what they ought for the sake of the fine, the temperate person's desires accord with his reason while the base desires of the continent person are contrary to his reason. Aristotle views the latter struggle as a sign of ethical immaturity and believes that it shows that the habituation process is incomplete— the continent person is not yet virtuous. If bad desires are coupled with weak reason, as in the incontinent person, they will even prevent good action. If they are coupled with strong reason, as in the continent person, they will not prevent correct action, but the action will not be done with full virtue. The continent person is deficient because it is not enough to recognize that the fine places an "ought" upon us; we must also desire the fine.

Earlier I described the problem with the continent person as a lack of unity. He is being pulled in different directions because he has not learned to desire rightly. He still views the three motivations as distinct. A related way of phrasing his deficiency is to say that his decision to pursue the fine is deficient. He recognizes how important it is to do the fine—he sees its obligatory force. But what truly motivates him? It is not the intrinsic loveliness of the fine, because he is not yet discerning that. At least, he is not yet seeing that it is much more lovable than everything else, and his other motives have not yet been transformed to harmonize with it. Rather, his internal conflict shows that he feels that the other objects of choice compete with it (even if he recognizes, rationally, that they cannot). In other words, he is not viewing the fine as higher than anything else, and he sees it as separate from what is pleasant and what is advantageous. To Aristotle, this means that his decision to pursue the fine is flawed. The continent person pursues the fine because he knows he ought to and because he knows it is worthwhile and part of the end, but not because he loves it more than anything else. His whole soul is not yet on board; his reason has gotten the point but the desires lag behind. And this means that his knowledge that "x is fine" is deficient. His relationship to the fine, then, should involve a combination of love and knowledge; he must know what it is and what it requires and he must love it because of what it is.

Furthermore, it is not enough to say that we want the fine and to know in a limited sense that the fine is the highest object of choice; we must truly know it, and there is reason to deny that the continent person does. Burnyeat is very helpful in spelling out this point: "I may be told, and may believe, that such and such actions are just and noble, but I have not really learned for myself (taken to heart, made second nature to me) that they have this intrinsic value until I have learned to value (love) them for it, with the consequence that I take pleasure in doing them" (1980, 78). In other words, the intrinsic value of the fine must be more than something that we are told about; it must be something that we experience for ourselves, a truth that we do not just accept but also experience and recognize as true.[21] And we cannot know this truth in this full sense unless we love the fine and have experienced its intrinsic value, which means that the continent person's knowledge is lacking. Of course, the same is true about the bad person. Indeed, his situation is much worse because he does not even believe that the fine has intrinsic value and does not see that he should aim at it.

BECOMING VIRTUOUS

If the lover of the fine is to express this love in fine action, he must know what the fine requires and have the strength to act accordingly. This means that he needs virtue of character and *phronêsis*. That is, he has to acquire good habits, tendencies to act, decide, and feel appropriately, and he must be able to figure out what to do. Otherwise, he would be what we might call a mere lover of the fine, somebody who loves the fine but is unclear about what it requires or is unable to do what he ought because he loves other things more and cannot avoid acting accordingly.

Aristotle explains that to become virtuous is to reach our end: "We are completed [*teleioumenois*]" when we acquire the virtues (1103a26). As Korsgaard succinctly puts it, virtue "is the perfected state of the human soul. It is the state in which a human being can perceive correctly, and be motivated by considerations of what is noble and good, and so can engage in rational activity" (1986, 277). Aristotle discusses the task of becoming virtuous in Book 2, noting that human virtue is twofold. Virtues of character belong to the desiring part of the soul and are acquired through habituation, and virtues of thought belong to the rational part of the soul and are acquired through teaching. I will argue that this division is not as sharp as it seems because virtue of character and *phronêsis* are closely intertwined. Virtue is a *hexis prohairetikê* which means that it requires reason. Our ability to make choices is a *hexis*, acquired in part through habituation, which means that habituation shapes our choice-making.

Virtue Is a *Hexis*

Aristotle defines virtue of character as "a state that decides [*hexis pro-hairetikê*]" (1106b36).[22] It is a state that decides how to act and, because it is an excellent state, it does so well. What does it mean to say that virtue is a *hexis*? Aristotle suggests that becoming virtuous is similar to becoming skilled at a craft (1103a32). By that, he explains, he means that in both cases we learn by doing. Just as we learn to build by building, we "become just by doing just actions, temperate by doing temperate actions, brave by doing brave actions" (1103b1). Virtue is "a state [of character that] results from [the repetition of] similar activities" (1103b20). In the beginning, we stumble and fumble. The process is long and tenuous. We make mistakes along the way. However, if we continually practice, we become better and better. The habituated person becomes somebody who is good at building or good at acting courageously.

If I have a *hexis*, I have a tendency to act in a particular way; I have a habitual action pattern. If I have the *hexis* of courage, for instance, I tend to act courageously. To say that virtue is a *hexis* thus suggests a certain regularity and reliability. The virtuous character is stable. We can trust her to act in a particular way. To say that virtue is a *hexis* also suggests certain ease. The good person does not have to struggle in order to be good. Forming tendencies to act is often very difficult; we have to repeat the action over and over again. But once that tendency is there, acting accordingly becomes much easier. Indeed, it often becomes virtually automatic (I will come back to this point).

But a *hexis* is more than a tendency to act in a particular way, because two people who tend to act in the same way can be in different states, one courageous and the other not.[23] I could regularly act like a courageous woman without myself being courageous. I might, for example, act to achieve honors in a society that places a premium on courage, or I might be continent, acting rightly but still struggling greatly to prevent my fears from driving me in the wrong direction. To have a *hexis* is also to have a tendency to decide and desire in a particular way (in our example, to do so courageously).[24] If I have a virtuous *hexis*, I love the fine. I do not merely do the right thing; I also do it for the right reasons and I enjoy doing it. In addition, my other desires must be appropriately ordered. Desires for honor or revenge are not necessarily bad but they must be subordinated to my desire for the fine, sometimes permitted and sometimes not. Underscoring the importance of desires, Aristotle writes that *hexeis* are "what we have when we are well or badly off in relation to feelings [*pathê*]. If, for instance, our feeling is too intense or slack, we are badly off in relation to anger" and we do not have the right *hexis* (1105b27). And to be well off means not just that we are able to control our feelings. That would be mere continence. Rather, our feelings must be in harmony with our reason. If I have to force myself to act according to a *hexis*, even if I do so habitually, I do not have the *hexis* but am still in the process of forming it. Finally, to have a virtue is to be able to discern what the fine requires in a particular area. If I am courageous, for instance, I can see what to do in situations related to courage, discerning what course of action would be courageous as well as what would be foolhardy.

Thus, to have a *hexis* is to have a tendency to act, feel, desire, and choose in a particular way. To be virtuous is to have a tendency to act, feel, desire, and choose correctly, in other words, to do so according to reason and for the sake of the fine. To have an individual virtue is to have a tendency to act, feel, desire, and choose correctly in a particular sphere. Courage, for example, deals with fear and confidence, and temperance with bodily pleasures. A virtuous *hexis* is formed through constant practice and once it is in place, performing virtuous actions is easy and pleasant (or at least does not involve pain). If I have a *hexis*, my decisions, desires, feelings, and actions accord with it. I can be relied upon to act in a particular way (courageously, temperately, and so on) and to enjoy doing so.

Virtue and Thought: Virtue Is a *Hexis Prohairetikê*

To say that virtue is a *hexis* that we acquire through constant practice seems to suggest that it is automatic and unthinking, a more or less blind habit. In spite of Aristotle's stated view that goodness requires both reason and desire, being good might seem to be almost exclusively a matter of appropriate desires, with reason playing the merely instrumental role of figuring out how to pursue ends acquired through habituation. On the contrary, reason plays a much larger role than that in both habituation and goodness because virtue is not just a *hexis* but rather a *hexis prohairetikê*, and because goodness requires that we be able to understand not just what to do, but also why a given action is right.

Let us begin by considering why saying that virtue is a *hexis* makes it seem so automatic and unthinking. Think about other things that we learn through constant practice. First, consider driving a stick shift car. I learned to drive on one so I find driving it quite easy. When I was first learning to drive, I was also able to explain what I was doing, in what order certain tasks had to be performed, and so on. Now that I am an experienced driver, however,

I cannot explain the procedures in any detail. I would not be able to teach somebody else to drive because in a very real sense I do not know quite what I am doing and in what order. When I drive, my body is simply performing the motions on its own.

Consider, also, performing particular techniques in a sport. For instance, I can execute a turning side kick in martial arts. If I stop to think about what I am doing, I might even be able to explain the steps of the kick to somebody else. However, my performing it well does not seem to require that I understand the reasoning behind the particular sequence of steps and that I grasp why each is important. I simply need to know what the steps are and to be able to perform them in a smooth, quick sequence.

Finally, think about solving certain types of mathematical problems. I can find the derivative of quadratic equations because I have a simple method memorized, and I know that the derivative is a limit because I have memorized that definition, too. This habit (of solving quadratic equations) does involve a certain amount of thought; if I did not think at all, I would not be able to find the answers. However, it involves only minimal thinking, basic subtraction and multiplication. I have no idea why my method works or, for that matter, what a limit is. Still, unless I am careless in my calculations, I get the right answer.

In all three cases, I am performing a task that I have learned through regular practice. Having been well habituated, I succeed almost every time. But I have little understanding of why I am doing what I am doing; I do not think much and I do not seem to need to. Still, I am good at driving stick shift, throwing turning side kicks, and finding the derivatives of simple quadratic equations. To become better, I simply need to practice more.

Now, Aristotle says that we become virtuous through habituation. Is he thereby suggesting that being good is very much like the model outlined above? Might being virtuous be a simple matter of being trained, getting one's feelings in check, and memorizing a series of steps? Does it require understanding or is it enough if we just know what to do and then do it? As Sherman notes, Aristotelian habituation has often been understood as mechanical and as "essentially separate from and antecedent to the development of rational and reflective capacities" (1989, 157).[25] And certainly, much of Aristotle's discussion in 2.1–3 reinforces this impression, as does the famous passage from Hesiod in 1.4:[26]

[We] begin from the [belief] that [something is true]; if this is apparent enough to us, we can begin without also [knowing] why [it is true]. Someone who is well brought up has the beginnings [*archas*], or can easily acquire them. Someone who neither has them nor can acquire them should listen to Hesiod: "He who grasps everything himself is best of all; he is noble also who listens to one who has spoken well; but he who neither grasps it himself nor takes to heart what he hears from another is a useless man." (1095b4–12)

This passage suggests that somebody can be noble simply by being well habituated and listening to and obeying his betters. However, as Aristotle's discussion continues throughout the *Ethics*, it becomes increasingly clear that this is not his view. Rather, the good person must make his own decisions, based on his own deliberation. In fact, this view is already visible in Book 1 where the good human life must be "some sort of life of action of the [part of the soul] that has reason [*praktikê tis tou logon echontos*]" (1098a3–4). The capacity for reason must be realized in action because *eudaimonia* is an activity, not a state or a capacity. It is hard to believe that an activity that is rational only in the sense of following directions and obeying could count as performing the human function well. Such activity, after all, can be performed even by a slave, and Aristotle is quite clear that slaves cannot lead a happy life. Rather, *eudaimonia* requires that I use my ability to deliberate and to make decisions about what to do. This is confirmed in 2.2 where he writes that "the agents themselves must consider in each case what the opportune action is, as doctors and navigators do" (1104a9).

And surely, the thinking involved in making good decisions must be much more complex than the thinking involved in my aforementioned mathematical exercises. One fundamental reason that this must be so is Aristotle's insistence that good decision making requires close attention to the particular case. Since every situation is at least slightly different, there could never be an algorithm that I could memorize which would help me act rightly: "Questions about actions and expediency, like questions about health, have no fixed answers" (1104a3–4). Consequently, it is not going to be possible to train the student by some sort of Pavlovian response drill (in situations of type A, do *a*; type B, do *b*; and so on). The number of possible situations is simply too large, and the relevant details of each situation are too many and too complex. Indeed, Aristotle argues that even when we know the specifics, figuring out what to do is very difficult: "In each case it is hard work to find the intermediate; for instance, not everyone, but only one who knows, finds the midpoint in a circle. So also getting angry, or giving and spending money, is easy and everyone can do it, but doing it to the right person, in the right amount, at the right time, for the right end, and in the right way is no longer easy" (1109a25–29). Thus, being a habituated person who automatically does certain things will not be good enough. As Sorabji puts it, "if someone is to become good-tempered, he must not be habituated to avoid anger come what may. The habit he must acquire is that of avoiding anger on the right occasions and of feeling it on the right occasions. . . . As a result, habituation involves assessing the situation and seeing what is called for" (1974, 216). It is not enough if the child learns to desire in the right way and to respond appropriately to certain stimuli; she also needs to learn how to think. A correctly educated person must be able to read the situation, figure out what to do and then do it. She must be able to evaluate the particular situation, determining if she should be angry, and if so how angry she should be, with whom, how her anger should be expressed, and so on.

By the time Book 6 focuses upon *phronêsis*, it is clear that goodness requires not only ethical but also intellectual virtue, namely *phronêsis*: "We cannot be fully good without *phronêsis*, or *phronimos* without virtue of character" (1144b32). The *phronimos* is able to "deliberate finely about things that are good and beneficial for himself . . . about what sorts of things promote living well in general" (1140a26). Thus, he does his own thinking—he does not just obey. As already noted, the crucial consideration in determining the person's worth is to look at his decisions: "It is by a man's *prohairesis* that we judge his character—that is, not by what he does but what he does it for" (*EE* 1228a4). A merely obedient person might be able to avoid badness but she will not be fully virtuous. To be virtuous, she must be able to figure out what to do on her own.

Now, one could try to preserve the unthinking simplicity of habituation by a division of labor, suggesting that becoming good is a two-step process. After all, Aristotle writes that "education through habits must come earlier than education through reason" (*Pol.* 1338b4) and speaks of a twofold process in which we first prepare the soul through habituation and then plant the seed of arguments and teaching (1179b24–26).[27] This suggests that we first acquire virtue of character, getting our desires into shape, and later start developing *phronêsis*. So perhaps habituation to virtue deals simply with the desiring aspect of decision, preparing the ground so that reason can add its contribution later. In further support of this view, Aristotle sometimes draws a sharp distinction between *phronêsis* and virtue, arguing that practical wisdom determines the means whereas virtue recognizes the end. In other words, we first acquire the ends through habituation—we learn to love the fine and to recognize the human end when we acquire the virtues of character. Then, in acquiring *phronêsis*, we develop our reasoning skills, learning how to figure out suitable means to these ends.

Aristotle's definition of virtue, however, rebels against this reading. As we have seen, Aristotle says that the virtues of character "are decisions of some kind, or [rather] require decision [*hai d'aretai prohaireseis tines ê ouk aneu prohaireseos*]" (1106a4) and that virtue is a "state that decides [*hexis prohairetikê*]" (1106b36). If virtue of character is a *hexis prohairetikê* and if it is acquired through habituation, then habituation to virtue cannot merely inculcate good desires. To have a virtue means that I will make good decisions and consequently that I will deliberate well. In other words, because virtue itself has a significant cognitive component, becoming virtuous must involve cognitive training. If I have good desires but cannot deliberate well, I do not have virtue of character. Development of virtue cannot be separate from and antecedent to the development of rational and reflective capacities. Aristotle cannot mean that we first acquire virtues of character through habituation and later learn how to make decisions when we acquire *phronêsis* through teaching. Rather, to be virtuous is to know how to make decisions.

It does not seem to be the case, then, that we first are habituated and then learn to reason, even though Aristotle sometimes does say so. Instead, the two processes must overlap. This suggests that while habituation and teaching (of *phronêsis*) are conceptually separate, they are either impossible or at least very difficult to pry apart in practice. We can see their close interconnections when we consider the difficulties involved in trying to keep virtue of character and *phronêsis* separated. Aristotle distinguishes them sharply in Book 2, but he blurs the lines between them in Book 6 when he argues that full virtue of character is impossible without *phronêsis*—and vice versa (1144b21).[28] They are necessarily coextensive. This too suggests that they must be developed at the same time. The educational program, then, must be one in which teaching and habituation are done together once we get beyond very early childhood.

KNOWING WHY

In order to be good, I need to be able to figure out what to do. Do I also need to understand the reasons for what I do? Is knowing the that (*hoti*) enough, or do I also need to know the why (*dioti*)? As Burnyeat notes, the distinction is between "knowing or believing that something is so and understanding why it is so" (1980, 71). In other words, to know the that is to know something simply because I have been told. It is the kind of knowledge that

I illustrated in my earlier discussion of derivatives and driving. If I know only the that, I know what I should do, but I do not know the reasons for which it should be done, beyond being able to say that it is right or fine to do so. Knowing the why, on the other hand, includes knowing the that but it also involves an understanding of the rationale for doing the that, providing a justification for it. Knowing the why of the derivative algorithm, for example, would involve knowing what makes my method work.[29]

McDowell suggests that in Aristotle's view "one does not need the *because* in order to shape one's life as one should; if one's grasp on the *that* is correct, and one acts on it, one will be living in accordance with virtue" (1995a, 212). The Hesiod passage (1095b4–12) does indeed suggest McDowell's position. Yet it seems clear that while someone who lacks the why certainly can live in accordance with virtue, he will not be virtuous.[30] To be virtuous, we need the why. Even in the Hesiod passage, Aristotle suggests that the person who himself grasps everything is best of all. It seems to me that when Aristotle says in the Hesiod passage that those who listen and obey are also noble, he has beginners in mind, which is appropriate since we are within the first few pages of the *Ethics*. Thus he writes: "We *begin* from the that . . . [W]e can *begin* without also [knowing] why" (1095b6–7, emphasis added). We begin—and must begin—by listening to others, thereby acquiring the that and a superficial grasp of the why. This is good enough for beginners. They will be doing the right thing by listening to the right people for guidance—exactly the right thing to do for somebody at their stage of development. Thus, they are noble. But they have not reached the *telos*; their development is far from complete. They are noble enough for beginners, but the very same level of understanding in somebody who should be more advanced is no longer noble because he should be able to figure out what to do by himself, and he should know the why. We expect more from the good man than from a beginner. The beginner is listening to reason, but he is not figuring things out for himself and is consequently not performing the human function. The good man is performing the human function well, which means that he himself is engaged in rational activity by figuring out what to do and why. Aristotle writes that the advanced man has been completed through virtue (1103a26) and is able to "grasp everything himself" and is therefore "best of all" (1195b11–12).

Consider the following passage from Aristotle's discussion of incontinence in 7.3:

Saying the words that come from knowledge is no sign [of fully having it]. For people affected in these ways even recite demonstrations and verses of Empedocles. And those who have just learned something do not yet know it, though they string the words together; for it must grow into them, and this takes time. And so we must suppose that those who are acting incontinently also say the words in the way that actors do. (1147a19–24)

Incontinent people know the that and they may even have a superficial why to offer. They are lacking because they do not act rightly. They are also lacking because in an important sense, they do not yet know. Like actors, they often say things without fully understanding them (and without being fully committed to their words). In one sense, they know what they are saying; they have the words committed to memory and can repeat them at will. But in another sense, and perhaps more important, they do not. The teachings they express have not yet become part of their stable character; they haven't had time to "grow into them." This growing into, it seems to me, is accomplished when the that is supplemented by a why, when we no longer just know what we should do but begin to understand the reasons for why that is so, when we start seeing why it is not an imposition but rather part of the good life.

What the force of this why will be is the question that will occupy us for the rest of the book. Will the why justify the that to any rational person or only to those who are already good? The next chapter will consider the disagreement between Kant and Aristotle concerning the proper role for desires in ethical decision making as well as Kant's related argument that empiricism cannot provide a sufficient why. As Kant himself puts it, "empirical principles are wholly unsuited to serve as the foundation for moral laws" (G 4:442). I will suggest that this is quite right; Aristotle cannot prove to the bad man that he should be ethical. His arguments will persuade only those who love the fine. Kant is mistaken, however, in believing that others can do better. If Aristotle is right to maintain that desire plays a crucial role in decisionmaking and in ethical education, as I will argue that he is, Kant is expecting too much. No mere arguments will sway the bad man, even if he is fully rational.

chapter two

THE KANTIAN CHALLENGE

I have suggested that the consequences of giving desire a crucial role in both our education and our adult goodness, as Aristotle does, are significant. More precisely, I have stated that such an emphasis on desire introduces serious limitations on what arguments can be expected to accomplish. In this chapter, I will continue to argue for this thesis by contrasting Aristotle's view of moral decision making with Kant's. (In this chapter, I will use "moral" and "ethical" interchangeably.) I will be using Kant to illuminate Aristotle's views on reason and desire, to help us understand their significance, and to prepare us for exploring the limitations of arguments on an Aristotelian view. I will often write as though Kant were responding directly to Aristotle and vice versa. Historically this is of course inaccurate: Kant rarely mentions Aristotle in his moral works, and his argument against eudaimonism focuses upon Stoics and Epicureans. Indeed, as Allen Wood notes, Kant probably had not studied Aristotle at any length (1996, 141).[1] Still, even though Kant does not say so, his criticisms of eudaimonism and empiricism have been taken to apply to Aristotle, and I will argue that some of them do.

After briefly summarizing the views of Kant and Aristotle regarding the role of inclinations (and desires), I will examine Kant's solution to "Hume's dilemma," which purports to show that morality can both motivate and bind, and its metaphysical implications. I will look at how, why, and to what extent Kant thinks that we can and should reform our inclinations, and contrast his view with Aristotle's. I will then discuss Kant's objection to actions that are motivated by good inclinations rather than by duty, and contrast Kant's and Aristotle's views of inclinations, bringing out the consequences of each one's view. In light of that discussion, I will turn to Aristotle's solution to Hume's dilemma, using it to illuminate Kant's and Aristotle's differing views of inclination and to emphasize the importance of the difference. Aristotle escapes the dilemma by refusing to accept Hume's dichotomy between reason and desire. But does he escape at the cost of being unable to explain why morality binds us? I will end the chapter by introducing the Kantian argument that Aristotle has no way of answering Thrasymachus; empiricism cannot explain the absolute bindingness of the moral law.

MORAL MOTIVATION: REASON AND INCLINATIONS

Aristotle's belief that inclinations can be formed and changed leads him to think that our understanding of what will make us happy can change and become ethical. If I am pleased by immoral action, my task is not simply to avoid acting on that inclination. That would be mere continence. For true virtue, it is also crucial that I retrain my inclinations. Indeed, the point of moral education is to get us to change and improve our inclinations. We are called upon to come to recognize that what is fine ultimately is advantageous to us and to recognize it as pleasant. Aristotle applies the term *phronêsis* both to reasoning about the advantageous and to moral thinking:

> *Phronêsis* is the science of what is just and what is fine, and what is good for a human being. (1143b24–25)

> It seems proper to a *phronimos* to be able to deliberate finely about things that are good and beneficial for himself. (1140a26–7)

In the beginner, so-called *phronêsis* can be self-interested (in a bad sense), focusing on getting whatever I want. I say "so-called" because the beginner's *phronêsis* really is not *phronêsis* but cleverness (*deinotês*). In the *phronimos*, however, *phronêsis* becomes *phronêsis* proper as he has come to view the fine as what he wants most of all. *Phronêsis* proper aims at the fine, but it is thereby also aiming at what one desires for oneself; it is still self-interested. Finally, *phronêsis* by itself cannot make any decisions, good or otherwise. All decisions are made by reason and desire working together.

In contrast, Kant argues that actions which are caused by inclinations lack moral worth. Consequently, ethical actions must be caused by reason alone. As we will see, he suggests that whereas we ought to train our inclinations to keep them from interfering with right actions, they must not be our motivation. To suggest that proper motivation is a combination of reason and inclination, as Aristotle does, is a terrible mistake:

> What is essential in the moral worth of actions is that the moral law should directly determine the will. If the determination of the will occurs in accordance with the moral law but only by means of a feeling of any kind whatsoever . . . and if the action thus occurs not for the sake of the law, it has legality but not morality. . . . [T]he [moral] incentive of the human will (and of every created rational being) can never be anything other than the moral law. (CPrR 5:71–72)

> The concept of duty thus requires of action that it objectively agree with the law, while of the maxim of the action it demands subjective respect for the law as the sole mode of determining the will through itself. And thereon rests the distinction between consciousness of having acted *according to duty* and *from duty*, i.e., from respect for the law. The former, legality, is possible even if inclinations alone are the determining grounds of the will, but the latter, morality or moral worth, can be conceded only where the action occurs from duty, i.e., merely for the sake of the law. (CPrR 5:81)

If we allow our actions to be motivated by inclinations, we destroy their moral worth. Reason and inclinations are radically different and they aim at radically different ends. Reason motivates moral thinking and aims at what is right; desire motivates prudential thinking and aims at happiness. This means that prudence and moral thinking can never become one and the same. Even if we can come to believe that being moral always is in our best interest, prudence and moral thinking will remain distinct because their motivations are and remain different—prudence is still linked to inclination and moral thinking to reason. Thus, it is a major confusion to use the same term to refer to both. Theories that assume that moral motivation is by inclination and not simply by reason distort morality and make it impossible.

KANT'S SOLUTION TO HUME'S DILEMMA: ACTION FROM REASON ALONE

Aristotle argues that reason by itself cannot make us act. Rather, desire and reason must work together. This does not mean that reason is a slave of the desires. While desires drive actions, they do not run the show in (fully) rational beings. We can step back from our desires and use reason to evaluate them, deciding whether or not we are going to act on them. Still, desires are necessary for action. My recognition that the fine requires a particular act cannot in itself motivate me; I must also desire to do the fine. And again, such desires are formed through proper habituation. Thus, habituation is crucial to goodness. Unless we somehow can make our inclinations and desires good, or are lucky enough to already have good inclinations, we are not going to be able to act well. Consequently, the first and necessary step in making somebody good is to begin modifying her feelings and inclinations, encouraging good ones and discouraging bad ones, fostering a love for the fine and a hatred for the base. Failing that step, the fine will not motivate, and we will not act finely because we will not know (in a full sense) what we ought to do. We might know that others want us to act finely, so we might act finely to please them, but we will not see the fine as something that concerns us and consequently will not act for its sake. The bad man is in precisely this situation.

But is it true that we become good in large part through habituation of our desires? Kant does not think so. In Kant's view, morality does not require moldable inclinations; it requires the possibility of action that is not motivated by desire. As Christine Korsgaard notes, Kant's project can be described as an attempt to dissolve the so-called Hume's dilemma by showing that morality can be both motivating and binding (1998).[2] Hume's dilemma is as follows: Morality must appeal to reason or to inclination, but since reason cannot provide a motive and inclinations cannot bind, morality can appeal to neither. If it appeals to our inclinations, it will motivate us to act, but it will not bind us because "I want to do y" simply expresses my preference and has no normative implications. Therefore, morality must appeal to reason. But then, the Humean argument continues, it cannot provide a motive to act. Let us say I recognize that I ought to do y. Here, we have a binding command. But surely, the recognition that I should do y, that I have an obligation to do y, does not suffice to motivate me? Kant attacks the dilemma at this point, suggesting that reason by itself can provide a motive for action. Or, to word this more carefully, if morality is possible, reason has motivating force. Henry Allison puts the point as follows: "Kant holds that we have a consciousness of the moral law as supremely authoritative for us; that this consciousness brings with it an incentive to follow its dictates that is totally independent of inclinations or desire (a pure moral interest)" (1990, 195). That is, through our consciousness of the moral law, reason generates a pure moral interest, which is not an inclination, and that moral interest is our motive for obeying the moral law. Furthermore, the moral law also generates a moral feeling which in turn generates sensuous motivation.

Kant agrees with Aristotle that we cannot act rationally without an end in view, and he goes as far as to say that we must be interested in an end (G4:387). However, as Allison notes, he distinguishes between having a desire, "which is a matter of nature, and being interested, which is (at least partly) a matter of freedom" (1990, 196). To deserve its name, Kant argues, morality must motivate us to act solely because we are rational and free beings. It must be possible for us to do something simply because we recognize that it is the right thing to do. That is, morality requires that we can transcend our inclinations and act spontaneously. We must be able to take a pure moral interest in something, an interest that is not contaminated by inclinations. If the empiricist analysis of human motivation were correct and complete, then reason could not set ends and make the human being pursue them without the help of inclination. And if that were so, Kant argues firmly, morality would be destroyed because autonomy would become impossible. Those who suggest that motivation is possible only through inclination and desire thereby encourage people to refuse human dignity by acting as if they could not help but always act on sensuous motives, as if heteronomy were the only option available to them, as if they were not moral persons.

Kant also expresses his point by noting that moral agency requires autonomy, the ability to act independently of, and sometimes contrary to, one's needs as a human being. As I argued previously, Aristotle insists that the good person must make his own decisions and act upon them. Kant agrees, but he takes the requirement much further, adding that an autonomous agent must self-legislate. And this, Kant argues, is possible only if her will has absolute spontaneity, if it is transcendentally free. Thus, Kant gives a non-naturalistic account of human agency. If I take myself to be a rational agent, I must think of myself as free in the sense of being absolutely spontaneous. That is, I must think of myself as being able to act on reasons rather than just being determined by my inclinations and other causes, and believe that each of my actions involves an act of spontaneity where I decide whether to go with my inclinations or with reason. And if I really *am* a rational agent, I must actually *be* absolutely spontaneous.

Aristotle agrees with Kant that freedom is necessary for morality. If I could not choose to act against some of my inclinations, deciding that they were not worth acting upon, I would not be a rational agent and hence not a moral agent. But for Aristotle, freedom is not equivalent to being able to act from reason alone. Goodness does not require the ability to act independently of all inclinations; it simply requires the ability to act as we see fit. And Aristotle does not see a problem here. Humans are obviously free to act as they see fit (at least sometimes), and it is equally obvious that their reasoning can influence their actions. Kant, on the other hand, lives in a world where Newtonian physics has made such freedom seem impossible. Experience yields compelling evidence for determinism because empirical experience shows us causally linked events, inclinations causing actions, chemical reactions causing inclinations, and so on. Thus, the ability of reason to cause change is utterly mysterious. In Kant's view, the mystery cannot be solved—we cannot understand the causality of reason. We can establish its possibility only through taking radical metaphysical measures: The possibility of spontaneity requires a move outside the natural realm. Human freedom and therefore morality are possible only on the assumption of transcendental idealism, the view that human beings must be viewed from two standpoints, as noumenal and as phenomenal, free and determined.

But does morality really require a noumenal realm and transcendental freedom? What generates the need for presupposing a noumenal realm and transcendental freedom seems to be Kant's insistence that morality requires actions from reason alone. If we adhere to the empiricist model of action, where inclinations help cause action, it seems possible to remain within a naturalistic framework. (However, we might escape the noumenal realm at an unacceptable cost. Kant argues that empiricism cannot explain the force of morality. We will return to this point later in the chapter.) Without being free in Kant's sense, we nevertheless seem capable of making the rational determination of whether or not to act on (some of) our inclinations and to follow reason (and other inclinations). Does morality, then, require the ability to make decisions that go against the dictates of each and every natural impulse that we have? Aristotle says no, and he is by no means alone in this view. Why does Kant believe that moral action requires action from reason alone? My first impression was that it was because he saw inclinations as completely determined, as events that happen to us and which are completely beyond our control. If they drive our choices, then, it means that our choice is driven by something which is beyond our control and that indeed seems to destroy morality. However, this cannot be Kant's train of thought because, as I will argue, he acknowledges that we can cultivate our inclinations in a more positive direction. Thus, they are at least to some extent within our control. But then, why must moral decision making and motivation exclude them completely? In the next sections, I will suggest that Kant's distrust of our inclinations and his acceptance of the dichotomy of reason and desire presupposed by Hume's dilemma underlie his conviction that morality requires the causality of reason.

REFORMING INCLINATIONS—WHY BOTHER?

Especially when reading the *Groundwork*, it is easy to get the impression that, for Kant, inclinations make no positive contribution to morality. On the contrary, a central purpose of morality seems to be to eliminate them. In an infamous passage, Kant writes that "the inclinations themselves, being sources of needs, are so far from having an absolute value such as to render them desirable for their own sake that the universal wish of every rational being must be, rather, to be wholly free of them" (G 4:428). We are twofold beings with a good and a bad part—reason and inclination. Reason bids us to be moral, but our inclinations continually distract us by demanding that we act for our own happiness, ignoring the end of morality and trying to use reason for their own purposes, turning moral reasoning into mere prudence, destroying autonomy and creating heteronomy, making us focus upon happiness instead of on morality. As human beings, we would perhaps regret the loss of inclinations, but as moral beings, we would be better off without them because they prevent us from acting morally. The moral task here is to make sure that reason—and not inclinations—runs the show:

> Since virtue is based on inner freedom it contains a positive command to a human being, namely to bring all his capacities and inclination under his (reason's) control and so to rule over himself, which goes beyond forbidding him to let himself be governed by his feelings and inclinations (the duty of *apathy*); for unless reason holds the reins of government in its own hands, his feelings and inclinations play the master over him. (MM 6:408)

In short, inclinations must be mastered and kept under control. Reason must rule the human being, keeping inclinations on a tight leash.

Now, Aristotle agrees that unruly inclinations are a problem and that reason must be in charge, but he suggests that we should solve that problem by teaching our inclinations to be moral; doing so is in fact an integral part of moral education which teaches us to mold our inclinations to harmonize with the fine. If we still have to fight inappropriate inclinations when we decide what to do, we have not learned as much as we should have. Thus, to Aristotle, the continent person who controls her unruly inclinations is only second best. The temperate person is better because she does not experience internal struggles. Rather, what she wants to do is what she should do; she enjoys doing the fine. Becoming that kind of person is a difficult task which only a select few will accomplish, but it is humanly possible and we lesser beings can at least get part of the way. It is true that the many will never transcend the struggle between reason and inclination. Still, many of us can become relatively continent, and a few can perhaps become temperate, achieving harmony between (good) reason and (good) inclinations.

How would Kant respond to this view? Roger Sullivan argues that Kant would reject Aristotle's position as unrealistic: "Kant thought that Aristotle's ideal of moral excellence and his analysis of practical wisdom were mere fantasy: We cannot habituate our emotions to love what is right (rather than what is merely pleasurable), as Aristotle had claimed, and if we could, we should not do so, since behavior based on emotions is heteronomous" (1994, 81–82n.10). On Sullivan's reading, then, Kant has two major concerns about teaching inclinations: First, he simply denies that it is possible to retrain our desires and inclinations to make them accord with what is fine (moral). To Kant, Sullivan argues, our inclinations are part of nature and as such they are determined and beyond our control. Second, he continues, even if it were possible to retrain our inclinations, focusing on that task would be misguided because moral actions ought not to be motivated by inclinations in the first place. Action motivated by desire is heteronomous and therefore lacks moral worth. Right desire does not improve a moral action; wrong desire does not detract from its moral worth.

I will argue that Sullivan is right in suggesting that one important difference between Aristotle and Kant concerns inclinations, but that the difference is not what he says it is. Sullivan makes it seem as though Kant believes that it is impossible for us to change our inclinations, and this is not true. It is true that Kant sometimes treats inclinations as though they are just there, inherently problematic and beyond our control. At other times (and this is surely his considered position), he allows for the possibility of changing inclinations. Indeed, as I will show in this section, he argues that we have an indirect duty to modify our desires and inclinations, trying as much as possible to bring them in line with the moral law. Thus, so far, Kant seems to be in agreement with Aristotle. However, disagreements soon reemerge. Kant argues that inclinations do not stay habituated; they swing back and forth. For this reason, making our inclinations good is a continuing struggle. In addition, as I will discuss in the next section, he argues that they do not improve the worth of an action. The reason for all of this, I will argue later, is that Kant denies that inclinations partake in reason. This means that Kant sees the training of inclinations as unthinking habituation, which is very different from Aristotelian habituation. The morally important features of a situation are identified by noticing where one's duty lies; nothing needs to be added. Thus, I am not increasing the moral worth of my action if, in addition to acting from duty, I also have feelings or inclinations which support that action. We cannot improve our understanding of a moral situation or our response to it by adding emotion and desire. The central reason for habituating inclinations, to the extent that it is possible, is to keep them from interfering, to prevent them from seducing us into violating the moral law. We must restrict (but not eliminate) our inclinations, getting them in line with morality, but not allowing them to determine our actions.

So how do we become good, according to Kant?[3] I have already discussed how Aristotle sees becoming good as a project of the habituation of our desires and acquisition of *phronêsis* and the improvement of our understanding of what the fine requires. It is a gradual development. In contrast, Kant argues that the decision to be virtuous "must be made all at once and completely" (*MM* 6:477). To become moral requires "a *revolution* in the disposition of the human being" (*Religion* 6:47). This is so because becoming moral involves changing our highest end from happiness to morality. As long as happiness is our highest end, all our projects are ultimately driven by self-love, and we are using prudence to get whatever we want. Our actions may still accord with morality, but they will lack moral worth because our motivation will be wrong. A gradual development from mere happiness-seeking into morality is impossible: "A disposition . . . to surrender at times to vice, in order to break away from it gradually, would itself be impure and even vicious, and so could bring about no virtue (which is based on a single principle)" (*MM* 6:477). There is no gradual road from evil to good; instead, there is a chasm that the agent must cross in a single leap.

However, it is not sufficient that our will alone change. Kant acknowledges the need for gradual habituation, suggesting that the revolution in our will must be accompanied by a gradual reformation of our sensuous nature, including our inclinations: "A revolution is necessary in the mode of thought but a gradual reformation in the mode of sense (which places obstacles in the way of the former)" (*Religion* 6:47). Indeed, he argues that we have an indirect duty to reform ourselves, bringing our sensuous nature into line with our will. And fulfilling this duty seems to include cultivating moral sentiments.

That we have a duty to reform ourselves should not be interpreted as optimism about our ability to become temperate in the Aristotelian sense. For Kant, getting our inclinations into permanently good shape is an impossible task because inclinations and emotions are fickle. Even if we do our best to mold them, they cannot be trusted. He strongly disagrees with Aristotle's harmonious picture of good human beings and presents the human situation as a never-ending battle, a "natural dialectic" where our desire for happiness constantly temps us to disregard our duty (*G* 4:405). In the *Metaphysics of Morals*, he describes us as "rational *natural* beings, who are unholy enough that pleasure can induce [us] to break the moral law" (6:379). Reason tells us to obey the law, but our desire for happiness and pleasure tempts us to ignore it—and too often we yield to temptation and act selfishly. Human beings, then, are torn between morality and prudence, reason and inclination. We are naturally inclined to act immorally, pursuing our self-interest over what is right; and even if we manage to be good, we can never get rid of this inclination. Allison expresses Kant's point well: "The moral agenda for finite, imperfect beings such as ourselves [is] to struggle to the best of our ability against an ineliminable reluctance to subordinate the requirements of our sensuous nature to the dictates of morality" (1990, 162). Even if we revolutionize ourselves, putting morality before self-love, this revolution remains reversible. At any moment, we might swing back in the other direction and fall back into self-love and evil. Reformation is an ongoing and uphill battle. We must reaffirm our commitment to goodness at every instance. We cannot trust our inclinations, even if they, at the moment, seem to be on the side of the gods. We have to struggle continually to control and reform them. Vigilance must never cease.

Because he believes that the struggle cannot be ended or won, Kant also believes that virtue always involves self-mastery or self-coercion. The virtuous person has to struggle with and control uncooperative inclinations (see Allison 1990, 163). Kant writes:

> *Virtue* is the strength of a human being's maxims in fulfilling his duty.—Strength of any kind can be recognized only by the obstacles it can overcome, and in the case of virtue these obstacles are natural inclinations, which can come into conflict with the human being's moral resolution. (*MM* 6:394)

Virtue signifies a moral strength of the will. (*MM* 6:405)

For a human being's moral capacity would not be virtue were it not produced by the *strength* of his resolution in conflict with powerful opposing inclinations. (*MM* 6:477)

Thus, Aristotle and Kant construe moral excellence quite differently. For Aristotle, virtue requires acting for the right reason and with the right emotion. From Aristotle's perspective, Kant's morality is one of mere continence, not temperance. Kant does not aim high enough; he does not recognize that good inclinations can become stable, that a human being can become virtually immune to temptation and corruption. He does not see that human nature can be perfected. From Kant's perspective, in contrast, Aristotle has an unrealistically high view of human nature:

> If a rational creature could ever reach the stage of thoroughly liking to do all moral laws, it would mean that there was no possibility of there being in him a desire which could tempt him to deviate from them, for overcoming such a desire always costs the subject some sacrifice and requires self-compulsion, i.e., an inner constraint to do that which one does not quite like to do. To such a level of moral disposition, no creature can ever attain. For since he is a creature, and consequently is always dependent with respect to what he needs for complete satisfaction with his condition, he can never be wholly free from desires and inclinations which, because they rest on physical causes, do not of themselves agree with the moral law, which has an entirely different source. Consequently, it is with reference to these desires always necessary to base the intention of the creature's maxims on moral constraints and not on ready willingness. (*CPrR* 5:83–84)

While Aristotle argues that temperance is extremely difficult, but in principle attainable, Kant concludes that temperance is entirely unattainable for human beings. Continence is the best we can do.

Still, virtue as self-mastery is not enough for Kant. He also suggests that we ought to reform our inclinations. But why is it not enough to simply control them, given that inclinations that are in harmony with the moral law do not increase our moral worth? I believe that part of Kant's reason for requiring such reformation is his recognition that many (most?) people will not act from the moral law. Given that, it is better that we act from inclinations that agree with the moral law. Then, we at least will not break that law, even if we fail to act from it. Reformation removes obstacles to moral action (*Religion* 6:48). However, Kant seems to view reformation of our empirical character as more than a way to prevent active immorality. He seems to regard it as a necessary correlate to the revolution in our will. Why? I believe that Kant recognizes that a person who truly has undergone a revolution of the will cannot reasonably neglect the reformation of his inclinations. To see why this is so, let us consider a person who has just made the leap over the chasm, committing himself to morality. What has he done? At a minimum, he has agreed to make morality his highest end and therefore to (try to) act morally whenever he is called upon to do so. Can he fulfill this vow without trying to reform his inclinations? I do not think he can. It is true that Kant argues that a good will is what counts, even if it is incapable of changing anything in the world: "A good will is good not because of what it effects or accomplishes, nor because of its fitness to attain some proposed end; it is good only through its willing" (*G* 4:394). This might suggest that a revolution in the will is enough and that reformation is unnecessary. However, Kant excuses the moral agent from the requirement of success, not from the requirement of doing his best. Directly following the passage quoted, he argues that the good will cannot be a "mere wish" but rather must be "the summoning of all the means in our power" (*G* 4:394). What does such summoning imply? At the very least, it seems to me, it implies that the revolutionized agent must try to remove anything he recognizes as an obstacle to moral action. Because it is so clear that inclinations often get in the way, this means that he must cultivate his character to prevent his inclinations from interfering with moral action. To adopt morality as the highest end is to recognize a duty to promote that end, and part of promoting that end is to bring my character in line. Thus, we have a duty to cultivate our characters, and Kant devotes the end of the *Critique of Practical Reason* to outlining "the method of founding and cultivating genuine moral dispositions" (*CPrR* 5:153).

If it is now clear why it is necessary for us to moderate inappropriate inclinations, it is less clear why it is also necessary to cultivate inclinations that support the moral law. Are they valuable as a means to avoiding immoral action because they provide a counterweight to stubborn bad inclinations, or does their cultivation have any independent value? The temptation is to use them as motivation for good decisions, but that is of course not acceptable to Kant. As soon as we let them influence our decisions, we seem to be destroying the worth of our actions: "Even to let other motives (such as those toward certain advantages) cooperate with the moral law is risky" (*CPrR* 5:72).

WHAT IS WRONG WITH ACTING
FROM GOOD INCLINATIONS?

Kant seems to be involved in a delicate balancing act. On one hand, as I just argued, he tries to make room for the view that character formation (including formation of inclinations) matters. We have a duty to cultivate our characters, becoming better people, so we must embark upon what sounds very much like an Aristotelian project. On the other hand, Kant still insists that moral action must be motivated by reason alone and that morality turns into prudence, and autonomy into heteronomy, as soon as we let inclinations become part of our motivation. It is obvious why we must not act from bad inclinations, but precisely what is wrong with acting from good inclinations? We will now look at Kant's reasons for not giving inclinations a role in determining the moral worth of an action and for arguing that the moral worth of an action is unaffected by the feelings and inclinations accompanying the action.

· Let us first turn to Kant's infamous examples in the *Groundwork* (G 4:397–99) which illustrate what it means to act from duty. Kant suggests that there are four types of action related to duty: An action might be (1) contrary to duty, (2) in accordance with duty and with mediate inclination, (3) in accordance with duty and immediate inclination, or (4) in accordance with duty and against inclination. I will focus on the last two, referring to the agents as the philanthropist and the dutiful person, respectively. In describing the philanthropist, Kant gives the example of people who are naturally sympathetic and who "find an inner pleasure in spreading joy around them" (G 4:398). Insofar as their actions are motivated by inclination rather than by duty, Kant argues, their actions lack moral worth. To describe the dutiful actor, Kant asks us to imagine the naturally sympathetic person having become depressed, losing that immediate inclination that used to drive him to act. Then, he asks, "suppose that, even though no inclination moves him any longer, he nevertheless tears himself from this deadly insensibility and performs the action without any inclination at all, but solely from duty—then, for the first time his action has genuine moral worth" (G 4:398). We get the same line of thought in the *Critique of Practical Reason*:

> It is a very beautiful thing to do good to men because of love and a sympathetic good will, or to do justice because of a love of order. But this is not the genuine moral maxim of our conduct, the maxim which

is suitable to our position among rational beings as men, when we presume, like volunteers, to flout with proud conceit the thought of duty and, as independent of command, merely to will of our own good pleasure to do something to which we think we need no command. We stand under a *discipline* of reason, and in all our maxims we must not forget our subjection to it. (*CPrR* 5:82)

Certainly actions of others which have been done with great sacrifice and merely for the sake of duty may be praised as noble and sublime deeds, yet only in so far as there are clues which suggest that they were done wholly out of respect for duty and not from aroused feelings. (*CPrR* 5:85)

As many scholars have pointed out, Kant is not suggesting that an action has moral worth only if one dislikes doing it.[4] His point, rather, is that an action has moral worth only if it is performed from duty rather than from inclination. Thus, actions that are in accordance with inclination have moral worth if they are performed from duty. In the *Metaphysics of Morals*, he even agrees that we should try to learn to enjoy doing our duty: "The rules for practicing virtue . . . aim at a frame of mind that is both *valiant* and *cheerful* in fulfilling its duties" (*MM* 6:484).

Yet, Kant presents the dutiful person described above as superior, and this seems objectionable. Is there not something morally significant missing in that dutiful person? Doing one's duty reluctantly certainly is better than not doing it at all, but am I not a better person if I do my duty gladly and does not such an act have greater moral worth? Furthermore, even if the philanthropist is not acting from duty, is it not wrong to deprive his action of all moral worth? Is there not something crucial missing in the motivation of the depressed man, which is contained in the motivation of the philanthropist? Does not wanting to help others make me a better person than somebody who has to force himself to help?

In trying to understand what is at stake here, Korsgaard's discussion (1996) is very helpful. She notes that both Kant and Aristotle believe that if we are to know that an agent's motivation was good, we must know both what the agent wants to do and why she wants to do it.[5] The dutiful man and the philanthropist want to do the same thing, namely to help, but their reasons for wanting to help differ; for one, it is duty, for the other, doing what he likes to do. And this, to Kant, illuminates what is wrong with the benevolent person. As Korsgaard explains, "The trouble with him is not that he wants to help others only because it pleases him to do so. The trouble is that he *chooses* to help others *only* because he *wants* to" (1996, 207). In other words, the helpful action for him only has external value; it is valuable only because it happens to please him. Essentially, then, he is acting out of self-interest, doing whatever pleases him. Thus, his motivation is selfish. In addition, moods are fleeting. When the philanthropist becomes depressed, we can no longer trust him to do the right thing. The dutiful person, in contrast, "chooses helping as her purpose *because* that is what she is required to do" (ibid.). Consequently, we can expect her to continue helping, no matter what her current mood is.

Now, as Korsgaard notes, the philanthropist and the dutiful person could be reflective or nonreflective, aware or unaware of the principle guiding their actions. The strongest feelings against Kant are generated when we are comparing the unreflective versions of each, comparing the person who helps impulsively, simply thinking that "[he] needs help" to the person who helps in "blind obedience to an abstract rule" (1996, 210). On the other hand, if we compare the reflective versions, the dutiful person who helps because he understands why helping is required seems morally superior to the person who helps because he knows it will make him feel good.

The more interesting comparison is between the two credible candidates for moral excellence, i.e., the unreflective philanthropist and the reflective dutiful person. Kant dismisses this philanthropist, as well, saying that she too is acting on the principle of self-love. Why is that? Kant seems to assume that there are only two possible principles of volition: morality or self-regard:[6]

All inclinations taken together (which can be brought into a fairly tolerable system, whereupon their satisfaction is called happiness) constitutes self-regard (*solipsismus*). This consists either of self-love, which is a predominant benevolence toward one's self (*philautia*) or of self-satisfaction (*arrogantia*). (*CPrR* 5:73)

The [moral] law rather imposes itself on him irresistibly . . . and if no other incentive were at work against it, he would also incorporate it into his supreme maxim as sufficient determination of his power of choice, i.e. he would be morally good. He is, however, also dependent on the incentives of his sensuous nature because of his equally innocent natural predisposition, and he incorporates them too into his maxim (according to the subjective principle of self-love). (*Religion* 6:36)[7]

Given that the philanthropist's motivation is not duty and that she is simply following her inclinations, then, she must be acting from self-love. And this also means that we cannot trust her to continue to act rightly. Once benevolent actions no longer please her, she will no longer perform them—unless she becomes motivated by duty. It is not enough to help when we are feeling sympathetic. We must help every time the moral law commands us to do so, and only somebody with a naively optimistic view of the kindness of a human heart believes that we always will feel sympathetic. Furthermore, if we believe that morality merely asks us to help when we feel like it, we are misunderstanding our relation to the moral law. We then "presume, like volunteers, to flout with proud conceit the thought of duty and, as independent of command, [we presume] merely to will of our own good pleasure to do something to which we think we need no command" (*CPrR* 5:82). Instead of seeing ourselves as volunteers, we must always remember that "we stand under a *discipline* of reason, and in all our maxims we must not forget our subjection to it" (ibid.).

THE NATURE OF INCLINATIONS AND WHY THEIR NATURE MATTERS

How is Kant's view of what makes an agent and action morally good different from Aristotle's? Aristotle, too, believes that we must look at both what the agent wants to do and why she wants to do it, and he agrees that an action has to be chosen in the right way to be valuable.[8] The agent must act for the sake of the fine. Aristotle also agrees that we can and should evaluate our inclinations, deciding whether or not to act as they suggest we should. It is not enough to do the right thing unreflectively; one must understand what one is doing and why that is what one should be doing. But in spite of this agreement, a crucial disagreement remains. And the disagreement here comes out when we ask whether actions with moral worth must be done with the appropriate feelings. That is, we are returning to Kant's fourth example—the dutiful man who acts against his inclinations. To Kant, this man is no less good than somebody who acts from duty and also enjoys it, and his act has no less moral worth. To Aristotle, he is inferior, and so is his action. But what is it that Aristotle and Kant actually are disagreeing about? It seems to me that the question of whether the dutiful man is lacking something important comes down to a question about the nature of inclinations and their relation to us.[9]

In Aristotle's view, our (habituated) inclinations make unique and relevant contributions to moral action and motivation. Proper perception of an ethical situation is in part emotional, and a proper response to it includes an emotional response. Inclinations are not irrational, but partly cognitive. They can be "persuaded in some way by reason, as is shown by correction, and by every sort of reproof and exhortation" (1103a1). The cognitive nature of inclinations means that reason can (and should) rule the inclinations by educating and molding them, seeking to persuade rather than to merely control them. And finally, it is clear why Aristotle gives so much weight to the project of changing our inclinations. Reformation of our character, which includes increased understanding as well as habituation of inclinations, simply *is* moral improvement. Habituation includes the process of increasing our perception by teaching the inclinations to see better. Without proper habituation, we cannot possibly be good.

To Kant, in contrast, as Korsgaard rightly points out, "pleasure and pain are mere feeling, [and] they are, to put the point a little bluntly, stupid"—and so are inclinations (1996, 225). My understanding of the situation is not affected by my emotional response to it. Training the inclinations is mere habituation of a dumb part of us. And, finally, while cultivation of inclinations is important for instrumental reasons, it is not the actual moral project, because it is possible for us to act morally even if we have not reformed our inclinations. What is truly important is the revolution of our will. Improved character is important to the extent that it enables us to do our duty. Depending on what our inclinations are like, it might be necessary to cultivate them. Still, moral improvement consists in adopting the moral end, not in reforming our character. Good inclinations and emotions have only instrumental value.

ARISTOTLE'S SOLUTION AND DISSOLUTION OF HUME'S DILEMMA

Kant solved Hume's dilemma of how morality can both motivate and bind by arguing that reason itself can motivate us to act. But, he also argued, to account for the possibility of morality, we must step out of the phenomenal realm in which our actions are determined by inclinations and other factors. We must assume that we are autonomous and therefore also transcendentally free. Thus, Kant operates with a dichotomy between nature and freedom. Aristotle's view of inclinations enables him to solve and dissolve Hume's dilemma in a very different way. Because Aristotle does not see inclinations as a stupid disturbance, in the way that Kant does, he does not see the need for action to be freed from them. For Aristotle, the step out of the natural realm to account for morality is both impossible and unnecessary—and so is Kantian autonomy. Aristotle explains how the fine can come to motivate by suggesting that we start with a *telos* that motivates us, an end which we naturally desire, namely pleasure. Then, we gradually learn, through being taught by our parents, teachers, etc., to change our understanding of *eudaimonia*, becoming motivated by an ethical *telos*, *eudaimonia* as properly understood. (I will discuss these two senses of *eudaimonia* in chapter 4.) The ability to be motivated by the fine is acquired through habituation.

Because he sees desires as intelligent, Aristotle also seems to dissolve the Humean dilemma by questioning its assumption that morality must appeal to reason *or* desire. As argued in the previous section, the desiring part is to some extent intelligent and thus it can be persuaded. Consequently, Aristotle stresses that reason's rule over desire is different from the soul's rule over the body (*Pol.* 1254b4–6). Unlike the body, the desiring part of the soul "shares in reason in a way, insofar as it both listens to reason and obeys it" (1102b31–32). This means that when it obeys, it does not obey blindly. It is capable of obeying reason willingly, agreeing with it, and is called upon to be part of the perception of the situation as well as the response to it.

Finally, Aristotle would undermine the dilemma in yet another way and this, I think, nicely summarizes the Aristotelian response to Kant. The dilemma gives two possible sources of action—reason and desire—and asks which of them generates moral action. In other words, it assumes that the two are separate or at least separable faculties. To Aristotle, they are not. The Aristotelian line between reason and desire is so blurred that the question about which one of them causes what no longer seems important. Aristotle says that "decision" can be described as a "*orektikos nous*" or as "*orexis dianoêtikê*"—desiring mind or thinking desire—and that the human being is the origin of such decisions (1139b4–5). Despite all his analysis in terms of faculties, Aristotle does not see reason and desire as fully separate. What is given and fundamental is their unity, namely the human being who makes decisions and acts, and she is found among the phenomena to be explained. McDowell puts it well: "The practical intellect [*phronêsis*] does not dictate to one's formed character—one's nature as it has become—from outside. One's formed practical intellect—which is operative in one's character-revealing behaviour—just is an aspect of one's nature as it has become" (1995b, 167). Both reason and desire are in the natural world, visible from the same standpoint. Reason exists in symbiosis with desire and cannot be separated from it, although it certainly can be thought of without desire. Thus, there is no need to protect reason and its decisions from contamination by contact with inclinations, and that is good because it is also impossible to do so. On the contrary, morality can be effective only by appealing to both reason and desire because human beings, those who are going to act and evaluate reasons for action, are comprised of both.

EMPIRICISM AND MORAL IMPERATIVES

Aristotle escapes Hume's dilemma, then, by providing an empirical account of human motivation whereby natural reason and desire together motivate ethical action. Reason and desire together recognize what we ought to do and our love for the fine motivates us to do it. Now, Kant would argue that Aristotle pays a steep price for escaping the dilemma in this fashion. If we unify reason and desire as Aristotle does, we will not be able to explain the force of morality. Empiricists like Aristotle cannot possibly explain why morality is binding upon all of us—they cannot explain categorical imperatives—and this is a disastrous failing because one of the central tasks of a moral theory is to account for our moral experience. As Aristotle might put it, a moral theory must explain the phenomena, including our beliefs about what morality is like. A theory that fails to do so is fundamentally flawed. Empirical or naturalistic attempts at explaining morality are thus doomed.

Kant argues, rightly I think, that the most striking feature of our moral experience is that we recognize the force of morality and its absolute bindingness. In the *Critique of Practical Reason*, he refers to our recognition that we always stand under the moral law as "a fact of reason" (*CPrR* 5:31).[10] He also argues that our experience of the moral law indicates that the law has certain characteristics. Most importantly, it is absolute rather than relative, and it expresses itself in categorical rather than hypothetical imperatives. That is, morality says "I don't care what you feel or want, you ought to do *x*," not "if you want *y*, do *x*." Even when we disregard the moral law, we still "recognize its authority" (*MM* 6:379). Thus, in order to account for moral experience, Kant argues, a moral theory must explain why morality binds us and why it has this absolute, uncompromising character.

In Kant's view, an empiricist theory cannot provide such explanations. More precisely, it cannot explain the force of moral imperatives. This is so because experience and empirical generalizations can only generate hypothetical maxims, and they are binding only if you want and care about the end they presuppose. If you love the fine, if you aim for *eudaimonia* understood as virtuous activity, you are motivated to act morally. But what if you do not? What in your empirical nature says that you must love the fine or care about *eudaimonia*? The answer seems to be "nothing"; we love the fine if we have been habituated properly, but if we have not, we do not. We can never find empirical evidence about human beings that can generate moral law and duty because something contingent and human cannot ground anything necessary and universal:

> Empirical principles are wholly unsuited to serve as the foundation for moral laws. For the universality with which such laws ought to hold for all rational beings without exception (the unconditioned practical necessity imposed by moral laws upon such beings) is lost if the basis of these laws is taken from the particular constitution of human nature or from the accidental circumstances in which such nature is placed. (G 4:442)

The moral law does not give hypothetical commands but, Kant argues, that is all empiricism can provide. Rather, its commands are categorical in that they "command for everyone, without taking account of his inclinations, merely because and insofar as he is free and has practical reason" (*MM* 6:216). In contrast, hypothetical imperatives only work on those who embrace the end they postulate. If I do not care about its end, or if I can find another route to it, the hypothetical imperative does not bind me.

One way of saving Aristotle from Kant's criticism would be to deny the need for moral imperatives and regard Aristotle as an anti-theorist who wisely resists the theoretician's (Kant's) demand for absoluteness and systematicity. On this view, Aristotle does not need absolute rules; he recognizes that what is needed is ethical perception, the ability to see what is needed in each, unique situation. But this approach does not seem fruitful because Kant seems to be right in arguing that ethics must include absolute rules—and Aristotle seems to agree. It is true that Aristotle is justly famous for resisting systematization and rules, for arguing as follows: "Every account of the actions we must do has to be stated in outline, not exactly. . . . [T]he type of accounts we demand should accord with the subject matter; and questions about actions and expediency, like questions about health, have no fixed answers" (1104a1–4). When it comes to our positive duties, determining when we should act courageously or temperately, or how angry we should get, we can give no answers that are both specific and universally applicable.

However, it seems to me that the apparent difference between Aristotle and Kant here is at least in part due to a difference in focus. Aristotle's discussion focuses on positive duties. He only mentions negative duties in passing, but when he does, his rules are as strict and as intolerant of exceptions as Kant's:

> The name of some [actions and feelings] automatically include baseness—for instance, spite, shamelessness, envy [among feelings], and adultery, theft, murder, among actions. . . . [I]n doing these things we can never be correct, but must invariably be in error. (1107a10–13)[11]

That is, Aristotle too needs room in his ethics for moral imperatives. He needs to be able to say that we *must* do certain things. But where does he get them and how does he justify them? What is the status of Aristotelian moral imperatives? Can we show the bad man that he should love the fine? The rest of this book will deal with these questions. I will argue that Kant is right in saying that Aristotle cannot explain why we are bound by morality, and I will begin by showing how the man of *theôria* whom Aristotle discusses in the *Ethics* can ignore ethics without thereby giving up *eudaimonia*.

chapter three

THE UNETHICAL
THEORETICIAN

As Kant points out, the problem with using hypothetical imperatives in ethics is that we can bypass them either by not being interested in the end or by finding a different means. If Aristotle tries to argue that "if you want to be happy (and because you are human you do), you must be ethical," he need not worry about the first possible escape because we are all interested in happiness, but the second escape creates a serious difficulty within the *Ethics* itself. Even though happiness is virtuous activity, the man of pure *theôria* can remain cold to ethics without giving up *eudaimonia* by arguing that he has found a different and superior way to be happy. The difficulty results from the twofold nature of virtue. Because wisdom is superior to virtue of character and *phronêsis*, the theoretician could perform the human function excellently by engaging in intellectual activity while ignoring *phronêsis* and thus be happy and yet unethical. It is tempting to agree with Kant here and say: "This is exactly what happens when you make something other than ethics more important. Somebody will neglect ethics and still get what is most important, and you are left with nothing to say against that person."

This issue is part of the more famous problem of how to reconcile the ethical and the contemplative life: Book 10 of the *Ethics* with its account of the contemplative ideal seems to undermine Aristotle's earlier defense of the ethical life (i.e., the life of virtue of character) by presenting a higher ideal whose relation to the ethical is not clear. Rather than being the *only* way of being happy, ethics seems to become merely *a* way, and an inferior one at that.

I will argue that the Book 10 emphasis on study makes explicit a tension inherent in the human function; hence, we cannot solve the problem by arguing that Book 10 does not properly belong to the *Ethics* at all.[1] Furthermore, I will argue, the supremacy of study does not render the ethical life without value, and it does not release the studying man from his ethical responsibilities—the fine retains its hold on him. Finally, I will suggest that while Aristotle denies that the unethical theoretician is happy, his argument for this view will have to rely upon premises from inside ethics that the theoretician need not accept. Consequently, the theoretician poses a serious challenge.

THE CONTENT OF *EUDAIMONIA—THEÔRIA* OR ETHICS?

The *telos* and the good for human beings is happiness, but what is the content of happiness? In Book 1, Aristotle uses the function argument to argue that the human good is "activity of the soul in accord with virtue" (1098a16). (I will discuss the function argument in chapter 4.) This definition is repeated elsewhere in the *Ethics* and also in the *Politics*:

Happiness is a certain sort of activity of the soul in accord with complete virtue. (1102a5)

The happy life is one in accordance with virtue and unimpeded. (*Pol.* 1295a34)

Happiness is the best thing, and this is the actualization of virtue and a certain complete practice of it. (*Pol.* 1328a37–38)

Happiness is the actualization and complete practice of virtue, and this not on the basis of a presupposition but unqualifiedly. (*Pol.* 1332a10–12)

Eudaimonia is virtuous activity. *Eudaimonia* requires virtue, but it is not identical to virtue—Aristotle was not a Stoic. He insisted that it is possible to be virtuous without being happy. This is so because virtuous activity requires more than just virtue. It also requires the appropriate external goods (such as friends, wealth, political power, and good birth). When Aristotle reformulates his definition of happiness in 1.10, he makes this requirement explicit:

Then why not say that the happy person is one whose activities accord with complete virtue, with an adequate supply of external goods, not just for any time but for a complete life? . . . We shall say that a living person who has, and will keep, the goods we mentioned is blessed, but blessed as a human being is. (1101a15–20)

Aristotle then explains that there are two sets of virtues—virtues of character and virtues of thought. Practical thinking about what to do, using *phronêsis*, and theoretical contemplation, using *noêsis*, are both important parts of happiness and of proper human activity. Excellence (*aretê*) in these two modes of thinking (*phronêsis* and *noêsis*) is made possible by the two types of human virtue (*aretê*)—ethical and intellectual, respectively. These two kinds of virtue in turn correspond to the two main aspects of human nature in Aristotle's account: We desire to know and we are social beings. In order to be happy, we need to indulge that desire to know, and we need to be with other people; we need a society and we need friends. In other words, we need to exercise both intellectual and ethical virtue in order to actualize human nature and to attain *eudaimonia*. The first nine books of the *Ethics* give great importance to the virtues of character and look very favorably upon the political life because such a life provides plenty of opportunity to exercise virtues of character.

In 10.7, however, the virtues of character and the happy life of exercising them are famously relegated to secondary status:

If happiness is activity in accord with virtue, it is reasonable for it to accord with the supreme virtue, which will be the virtue of the best thing. The best is understanding . . . and to understand what is fine and divine, by being itself either divine or the most divine element in us. Hence complete happiness will be its activity in accord with its proper virtue; and we have said that this activity is the activity of study. (1177a13–17)

The best life, the life of most complete happiness, is now a life of *theôria*. Ethical virtue provides only a lower form of happiness:

[The theoretical] life, then, will also be happiest. The life in accord with the other kind of virtue [i.e., the kind concerned with action] is [happiest] in a secondary way, because the activities in accord with this virtue are human. For we do just and brave actions, and the other actions in accord with the virtues, in relation to other people, by abiding by what fits each person in contracts, services, all types of actions, and also in feelings; and all of these appear to be human conditions. (1178a9–14)

These chapters do not deny that the ethical life is happy and worthwhile; Aristotle is simply saying that the theoretical life is better and happier. He still seems to think of a life of ethical virtue as happy. However, it is clearly inferior to the theoretical life.

What happens to the picture of *eudaimonia* that had been presented in the first nine books of the *Ethics* when the theoretical ideal is introduced? Does not the claim that the happiest life is theoretical undermine ethics by suggesting that those who theorize can ignore ethics and still be happy? How important is ethics, really, at the end of the *Ethics*? Some thinkers, including Annas and Nussbaum, have argued that this is an unnecessary question because the two accounts belong to different points in Aristotle's intellectual development. Annas writes:

> I have not in this book touched on the endlessly discussed question of whether Aristotle's "intellectualism" in Book X is consistent with the rest of the work. My own view is that the problem is a spurious one, since the *Nicomachean Ethics* as we have it is not a work which Aristotle wrote, which "Book X" and the other books are part of. . . . There is no reason to expect these collections [of lecture notes, put together by Andronicus] to be unified like a modern book (there are several ways, not just this one, in which they are not) and thus no reason to try to harmonize texts as different as the ones we call "Book I" and "Book X." (1993, 216n.1)

Nussbaum expresses a very similar view:

> What we can say with confidence is that these chapters [*Ethics* 10.6–8] do not fit in the argument of the [*Ethics*]; indeed, that they represent a line of ethical thought that Aristotle elsewhere vigorously attacks. With only slightly less confidence, we can also assert that they do not fit well in their context, and were probably composed separately. (1986, 377)

When trying to understand the argument of the *Ethics*, then, we can omit 10.6–8.

I find the developmental solution deeply unsatisfactory because the tension between the two ideals is present throughout the *Ethics*.[2] In Book 1, Aristotle suggests that there are three popular candidates to the happy life, namely pleasure, honor (or virtue), and study (*theôria*) (1095b17). He then postpones the discussion of the life of study (1096a6), promising to deal with it later, a promise that he does not fulfill until Book 10. Thus, without Book 10, that promise would remain unfulfilled, and the *Ethics* would seem incomplete (especially given the Platonic intellectual context in which Aristotle operated). The conclusion of the function argument also suggests the possibility of one virtue that is higher than all others; Aristotle writes that the human good is the activity of the soul in accord with virtue "and indeed with the best and most complete virtue, if there are more virtues than one" (1098a17).[3]

Furthermore, the conflict between the two lives seems inherent in the dual structure of human virtue and function. Aristotle introduces two types of virtue (virtues of thought and virtues of character) in 2.1, linked to the rational and the desiring part of the soul, respectively. He notes in 6.1 that the virtues of thought also are of two kinds, corresponding to two parts of the rational soul. The scientific part (*epistêmonikon*) discovers principles of things which cannot be otherwise—using *epistêmê* (scientific knowledge), *sophia* (wisdom) and *nous* (intuition)—while the rationally calculating part (*logistikon*) deals with principles of things which could be otherwise—using *technê* (craft) and *phronêsis*. Reconciling *phronêsis* and virtue of character involves no great difficulty because Aristotle insists that they are coextensive, if not identical: "One has all the virtues if and only if one has *phronêsis*" (1145a2). In contrast, excellence in *sophia* and in *phronêsis* seem to be separate and separable: Aristotle speaks about Anaxagoras and Thales, citing and seemingly agreeing with the common view that they were wise but lacked *phronêsis* (1141b1–5).[4] Pericles has *phronêsis* but there is no indication that he has *sophia* (1140b9). Confirming the suspicion that the two modes of thinking are separable, Aristotle suggests in the *Politics* that we must choose between philosophy and politics. Those who can do so hire an overseer to take care of the household while "they themselves engage in politics or philosophy" (1255b35–37). Furthermore, he notes that the right decision to make when faced with the choice between the two is subject to discussion:

> There is a dispute among those who agree that the most choiceworthy way of life is that accompanied by virtue as to whether the political and active way of life is choiceworthy, or rather that which is divorced from

all external things—that involving some sort of study, for example—
which some assert is the only philosophic way of life. For it is evident
that these two ways of life are the ones intentionally chosen by those
human beings who are most ambitious with a view to virtue . . . the
two I mean are the political and the philosophic. (1324a25–33)

Thus, it is not just that it is possible to have *phronêsis* without *sophia* and
vice versa. It is also impossible or at least hard to focus successfully upon
both. We seem to be forced to choose between lives devoted to one or the
other. Should we try to live like Anaxagoras or like Pericles? Should we focus
upon philosophy or politics, *theôria* or ethical virtue? Returning to Book 1, we
can see that this tension is inherent in the very definition of happiness.
Excellent activity according to *logos* distinguishes the excellent man and constitutes happiness, but we now know that such activity is performed in two
spheres, by *sophia* and *phronêsis*, respectively. Indeed, the very function
of man—rational activity—is twofold, and well before Book 10 the *Ethics*
calls out for a way of adjudicating between the demands of each in case
of conflict.[5]

Due to the above considerations, it seems clear that the conflict between
the two ideals is present in the *Ethics* even if we omit Book 10. We therefore
face a choice: Either we excise all the passages which present the contemplative view or the dual nature of virtue and function and we provide textual
reasons for doing so, or we try to understand how Aristotle thought that
humans could and should pursue both the ethical and the contemplative
ideals. I find the first solution ad hoc, and I also believe that it gives up too
soon. If we assume that passages that are difficult to reconcile simply do not
belong together, we might neglect avenues that would deepen our understanding of Aristotle. Thus, in the absence of compelling evidence that the
relevant passages should be excised, we should try reconciliation first.

I will argue that Aristotle clearly thinks that the best life, without qualification, is a life of actualization of knowledge, exemplified by the divine life.
However, due to our limitations, that life is not the best life possible for
human beings. Rather, the best possible life for human beings is a life of
study, in which some knowledge is actualized but most of our time is spent
pursuing more knowledge. But even that life is too high for many human
beings; for them, the best thing to do is to focus upon living an ethical life.
The people who are capable of living a life of study have to face the conflict
between the theoretical and the ethical life. Finally, I will argue that, according to Aristotle, even though *theôria* is the supreme activity, ethics should

retain its force, and most of those who study will be called upon to abandon their theoretical activity—for short periods of time or for their entire life—in order to fulfill their ethical commitments.[6] Thus, the tension between the theoretical and the ethical ways of life is potentially or actually present in every human life.

WHAT IS THE LIFE OF *THEÔRIA*?

Aristotle's argument in 10.7 and 10.8 concludes that the unqualifiedly best life and the best activity is that of divine *theôria*. What sort of life and activity might that be? In the *Metaphysics*, Aristotle explains that the divine life, which is the best life of them all, is a life of eternal self-contemplation. Recall that haunting portrait in Book Lambda of God thinking himself, or of thought thinking itself always and eternally:

> It is of Himself, then, that The Intellect is thinking, if He is the most excellent of things, and so Thinking [*noêsis*] is a thinking of Thinking. (*Met.* 1074b33–35)

> Thinking is the thinking [*noêsis*] of Himself through all eternity. (*Met.* 1075a10)

God is not learning or studying because he already knows all that is worth knowing for him. Instead, God turns away from the world and contemplates himself. It is a proper activity—indeed, the only proper activity—for the Aristotelian deity.

Now, somehow, this divine *noêsis* is supposed to serve as a *telos* for us—and for every other living creature.[7] The better we approximate divine activity, the happier we will be: "And so the human activity that is most akin to the gods' activity will, more than any others, have the character of happiness" (1178b24). Most life can mimic God only by reproducing.[8] Humans are special because by engaging in thought in general and in *theôria* in particular—*theôria* is *nous* plus *epistêmê* (1141a19)—we are able to engage in the same activity as God, namely noetic activity, thus approaching God much more than any other living creature can. We cannot become gods but we should try to do so, and our life will improve to the extent that we succeed in living a divine life. Focusing on lesser things will reduce the quality of our life:

We ought not to follow the makers of proverbs and "Think human, since you are human," or "Think mortal, since you are mortal." Rather, as far as we can, we ought to be pro-immortal, and go to all lengths to live a life in accord with our supreme element. (1177b32–35)

The admonitions to avoid human and mortal thoughts bring to mind St. Augustine's argument in the *Confessions* against natural science, which suggests that we are wasting our time if we are studying the world rather than contemplating God:

Who can tell how many times each day our curiosity is tempted by the most trivial and insignificant matters? Who can tell how often we give way? . . . I no longer go to watch a dog chasing a hare at the games in the circus. But if I should happen to see the same thing in the country as I pass by, the chase might easily hold my attention and distract me from whatever serious thoughts occupied my mind. . . . Unless you made me realize my weakness and quickly reminded me, either to turn my eyes from the sight and raise my thoughts to you in contemplation, or to despise it utterly and continue on my way, I should simply stop and gloat. (10.35)

Based on the passages cited above, Aristotle seems to take a position similar to the one expressed by St. Augustine: we should spend our lives contemplating God, thereby imitating God as much as we can. Only thus do we make ourselves as immortal as we can; only thus do we lead the happiest life. It seems it is not enough to be learning; instead, we should contemplate what we already know, and the object of our contemplation should be an elevated one.

Now, Aristotle seems to spend very little time thinking about God. Indeed, he falls prey to "excessive curiosity" about the natural world much more than Augustine ever did, driven by his interest in what by comparison to the divine are minute details and unimportant things, "wasting" time dissecting animals, examining various forms of civic constitutions, and so on. Does this mean that Aristotle thinks that he is living an inferior life? He clearly thinks that a human life is inferior to that of a god, but I find it hard to believe that he thinks that he is living an inferior human life. On the contrary, I suspect that he thinks he is leading the best life possible for a human being. How is that possible, given that he is so frequently studying frogs rather than gods?

The solution, I think, is to notice that by studying frogs and other natural things, Aristotle is in fact studying God—or at least godlike things. At first, this might sound absurd, but the absurdity evaporates when we realize that the division between mortal and immortal, worldly and divine things, is not as sharp as it might at first appear. Objects of *theôria* have to be necessary, unchanging, and eternal. This might lead us to think that there is *theôria* only about gods, stars, and mathematical objects. However, in the *Eudemian Ethics*, Aristotle explains that we engage in *theôria* about things in the world as well, when we seek to uncover their nature and cause (*to ti* and *to dia ti*) (1216b38). A cursory look through the corpus shows that we can have *theôria* about a diverse group of items: sensible substances, substances but not accidents, the sensible and the eternal, all beings, things, *archai*, mathematical truths, truth, music, and the modes of speech. That is, we can study the eternal and unchanging aspects of changing things.[9] In grasping their nature, we engage in *nous*—the divine activity and one of the two parts of *theôria*. Furthermore, because the knowable parts of each thing are eternal and unchanging, they are thereby like God. Finally, our study of the causes of things in the world must include a study of God because God is the final cause of all things. And, it seems, understanding the striving of mortal things to become divine is an essential part of understanding what they are.[10] Thus, by studying the things of the world, we are, in a sense, engaging in the same activity as God, and we study what, in the world, is most God-like.

There is yet another way in which the human life of study and contemplation must be different from that of God. We must distinguish between what is the best life per se and what is the best life for beings with our particular limitations. They are not identical. Aristotle says that the best life is "superior to the human level" (1177b27). He spells out the crucial distinction in the *Politics*:

> Actions stand in a comparable relationship: those belonging to that [part] which is better by nature are more choiceworthy for those who are capable of achieving either all of them or [those belonging to] the two [lower parts]. *For what is most choiceworthy for each individual is the highest it is possible for him to achieve.* (Pol. 1333a27–30, emphasis added)

The life of a God contemplating himself always and forever is the best life per se. However, even though that is the best life, we would not be living the best life possible for us if we tried to live exactly such a life. We are not the best kind of beings, and the most choiceworthy life for us is the highest life that is possible for us, not the highest life per se. Mimicking God, then, is not trying to live a life exactly like God's but rather trying to live the best life possible for us. But what life is that? What sort of contemplation or knowledge seeking does it involve?

In Aristotelian terms, we can distinguish between four stages of knowledge. First, we know a thing potentially; that is, we do not know it yet, but we have the capacity to learn about it. Second, we are seeking knowledge, or are learning, thus moving from potential to actual knowledge. Third, we know but are not currently thinking about it. And fourth, we contemplate what we know. Divine *noêsis* is, of course, on the fourth and highest level. Aristotle is very clear that the life of the knower is better than that of the seeker: "It is reasonable for those who have knowledge to spend their lives more pleasantly than those who seek it" (1177a26). "All men begin, as we said, by wondering that things are as they are. . . . But we must end with the contrary and, according to the proverb, the better state, as is also the case in these instances when one has learned the cause" (*Met.* 983a18–19).

Now, given that knowing is superior to seeking, should we not focus upon contemplating what we know rather than on learning more? The answer, it seems to me, is no. If we assume that the best life for a human being is a life of knowing rather than seeking because a life of knowing is better, we are forgetting the lesson from the *Politics* passage above about not confusing the best life per se with the best life for us. The best life for us takes into account that we are born in ignorance. Consequently, if we are going to imitate God, we need to become more knowledgeable, which means that we must seek. Before humans become knowers, we must be seekers. The life of contemplation of what we already know can at most be a life at the endpoint for us. A life of contemplating God is a life for a being who is beyond us, namely, one who already knows and has ceased to wonder. When we have become like gods, when we have learned all there is to know or all that is worth knowing, all that remains is to sit back and contemplate these things. While we remain human, the world is there, calling out to be known.

Of course, knowledge is not an all-or-nothing matter. As we grow and learn, we come to know some things while remaining ignorant of others. There is a long continuum between the ignorant baby and the being who knows all and, once we know a reasonable amount, giving up study and instead contemplating what we have learned becomes possible. What is a reasonable amount? At what point should we stop seeking and start living the life of a knower in order to live the best life? When we have learned half? Twenty percent? Five? Since we can never become all-knowing, this "before we know all" will last our entire lifetimes. So should we be contemplating what we already know, or should we continue to expand our knowledge? Aristotle does not say, but judging from his actions he believes that we are better off continuing to seek. It seems to be more important to him to expand his knowledge and to teach others what he knows than to contemplate what he already knows (although perhaps teaching should be viewed as a form of contemplation). The best life for beings in our condition of relative ignorance is one of knowing while also seeking to know more. The life of pure contemplation suits the one who has already understood everything, but it does not suit us. To imitate God, then, is to lead the best life we can, namely a life of thinking and learning.

WHAT DEMANDS DOES ETHICS PLACE ON A PERSON WHO IS ABLE TO THEORIZE?

Now, what relation does the life of study and contemplation have to ethics? The crucial question to ask in order to understand Aristotle's position on the relation between ethics and *theôria* is: What demands does ethics place on a person who is able to theorize? Some commentators ascribe a very worrisome answer to Aristotle, in which *theôria* attains absolute supremacy and silences all ethical requirements. (I suspect that worries about this result might be part of the reason why Nussbaum, Annas, and others want to get rid of the contemplative ideal altogether.) Is Aristotle suggesting that for those of us who are capable of leading a contemplative life, the fine no longer provides a reason for action, either in choosing a life path or in choosing immediate action? Or—a little milder—is he saying that it no longer provides a reason that can count against contemplation? Might it silence lower considerations, including ethics, just as ethics (itself) does? Cooper argues for *theôria* silencing ethics in *Reason and Human Good in Aristotle* (1975). (He changed his mind later [1987]). Similarly, Wilkes writes: "The 'philosophic' life ultimately denies all value to the 'political' one; the conflict could not be more pointed. . . . [O]ne cannot, and should not try to, juggle with the texts so that the conflict of the two lives is resolved" (1978, 351).

A few passages do in fact suggest that Aristotle thought that *theôria* could and should silence ethics. As Wilkes notes, Aristotle writes:

Whatever mode of choosing and of acquiring things good by nature—whether goods of body or wealth or friends or the other goods—will best promote the contemplation of God, that is the best mode, and that standard is the finest; and any mode of choice and acquisition that either through deficiency or excess hinders us from serving and from contemplating God—that is a bad one. (*EE* 1249b15–22)

He expresses similar sentiments in the *Ethics*, Book 10:

Happiness extends just as far as study extends, and the more someone studies, the happier he is, not coincidentally but insofar as he studies, since study is valuable in itself. And so [on this argument] happiness will be some kind of study. (1178b30–34)

Insofar as he [who studies] is a human being, however, and [hence] lives together with a number of other human beings, he chooses to do the actions that accord to virtue. (1178b5)

Theôria alone seems to be liked because of itself, since it has no result beyond having studied [*Doxai t'an autê monê di' hautên agapasthai: ouden gar ap' autês ginetai para to theôrêsai*] (1177b2, my own translation)[11]

Taken in isolation, these passages suggest two claims: (1) the theoretical life and activity is the best, and (2) all others are valuable only insofar as they aid the higher; they are only for the sake of the higher. Combining these claims, we find that ethical actions no longer seem to be important for their own sake. Rather, the theoretician would act ethically only when it is necessary for *theôria*. Fine actions become mere means. Because the philosopher lives in the city, he chooses to act virtuously, but he is no longer motivated by the fine in ethical actions. His actions, then, are not really ethical; they lack the proper motivation. The intrinsic value of ethics is eliminated.

In my view, believing that Aristotle would willingly let *theôria* undermine ethics is a mistake. Aristotle did not view the first nine books as a ladder to climb and then throw away once we have reached the wisdom of Book 10. The earlier books still pertain at the end of Book 10. Virtues of character do have intrinsic value and must not be turned into mere means. The first passage, the one from the *Eudemian Ethics*, raises legitimate worries about authenticity. Can we really attribute a passage that tells us to serve God to

Aristotle? Exactly how does one serve a god who is not even aware of our existence? Is this not a Christian thought that must have been inserted by somebody else? Or is it a thought more suitable to a traditional Greek (rather than an Aristotelian) understanding of the gods? And if we take the requirement of service to be a later extrapolation, might we not do the same with the rest of this passage? If we read them in the context of Aristotle's overall view, the other three passages can be explained without assuming that Aristotle allowed the theoretical man to give up ethics.

The claim that the philosopher stands outside the realm of ethics ignores Aristotle's account of how we become ethical and when we become philosophers. It seems clear that it is a temporal succession in play here. First we develop ethical virtue, and then we become philosophers: "Education through habits must come earlier than education through reason, and education connected with the body earlier than education connected with the mind" (*Pol.* 1338b5–7). A passage in the *Ethics* points to the same conclusion: "Virtue of thought arises and grows mostly from teaching, that is why it needs experience and time" (1103a15). This means that the person who turns to *theôria* already should be ethical. His character should have been shaped to have desires and love for the fine and to enjoy doing the right thing. His good habits should be in place; his desires ought to be shaped; his character should be formed. For the philosopher to be unethical would require an undoing of the ethical character he has acquired. (However, notice that I say "ought" and "should" here. The possibility of somebody who has not been properly educated towards the fine living a life of excellent rational activity [*theôria*] seems to remain. We will turn to this person at the end of the chapter.)

The question, then, is whether there is any reason to think that *theôria* would undo and undermine ethics, if it would lead to the philosopher rehabituating himself, abandoning the old desires, habits, and character and, perhaps more importantly, becoming convinced that the *phronimos* is wrong about what ought to be done. In some forms of Hinduism (I am thinking especially of Advaita Vedanta), the person who attains *moksha* discovers that all distinctions are unreal, including the distinctions between good and bad, right and wrong. He sees that ethics is founded on distinctions that do not have the absolute value and truth that is claimed for them, and he recognizes that he no longer is bound by ethics. But there is no reason to think that Aristotle believes that *theôria* will lead to such an insight. *Theôria* does not undermine what the *phronimos* (man of practical wisdom) knows. Things really are as they appear to the *phronimos*; the *phronimos* sees correctly:

Phronêsis is a state grasping the truth, involving reason, concerned with actions about things that are good or bad for a human being. (1140b5)

These [older] people see correctly because experience has given them their eye. (1143b14)

Theôria does not overturn our habituation, changing the structure and direction of our desire to remove this love and desire for the fine. Study will add another desire, namely that of spending our time studying, but it will not overturn the intrinsic value of ethical action.[12] The fine remains in place as a reason for action and, I will argue, with power to overrule other reasons, including the reason that I want to study because I want to lead the best life.

But if *theôria* is higher than ethics, how can ethics ever outweigh *theôria* when they are in conflict? As Sherman puts it, "if [*theôria*] is the perfect and best way to spend time, then why should we not maximize it in a life, and make it an end which all other ends subserve? Why not promote morality as merely a condition of contemplation?" (1989, 100). Even if ethics remains good, is not *theôria* better and hence always preferable? I think Aristotle would respond by first noting that humans live in a community with friends, relatives, and others:

Man is by nature a political animal. He who is without a city through nature rather than chance is either a mean sort or superior to man. . . .
One who is incapable of participating [in the activities of the city] or who is in need of nothing through being self-sufficient is no part of a city, and so is either a beast or a god. (*Pol.* 1253a1-2, 28–29)

People who can live without such a community are not human but rather beasts or gods. Gods may not need justice, temperance, and friendship, but we do because we need other people.[13] Why do we need and want to live in a community? There seems to be a couple of different reasons. First, we are not fully self-sufficient. In order to pursue *theôria*, indeed in order to live, the philosopher needs to be in a community so that the necessities of life can be provided:

But happiness will need external prosperity, also, since we are human beings; for our nature is not self-sufficient for study, but we need a healthy body, and need to have food and the other services provided. (1178b33–36)

Insofar as he is a human being, however, and [hence] lives together with a number of other human beings, he chooses to do the actions expressing virtue. Hence he will need the sorts of external goods [that are needed for the virtues], for living a human life. (1178b5–7)

Presumably, however, one's own welfare requires household management and a political system. (1142a10)

In order to secure the necessities of life, the philosopher chooses to live in a city. He will therefore be motivated to make sure that people keep some sort of peace with each other—it is difficult to theorize in the middle of civic unrest. This might include helping to rule or following the laws to set a good example.

Thus, part of the reason philosophers lead ethical lives is simply self-serving. But although the above passages do not make it clear, that is not the only reason. To choose to do virtuous actions is not to respond to a personal whim; it is a matter of recognizing the right course of action. Aristotle insists that the community, the *polis*, has primary importance: "One ought not even consider that a citizen belongs to himself, but rather that all belong to the city; for each individual is part of the city" (*Pol.* 1337a27–29).[14] Similarly, in the *Ethics* he writes: "While it is satisfactory to acquire and preserve the good even for an individual, it is finer and more divine to acquire and preserve it for a people and for cities" (1094b9–11). The supreme importance of the city is also suggested by the fact that Aristotle turns to the concerns of the city after he discusses *theôria*. If *theôria* made the city unimportant, Aristotle should have ended the *Ethics* after 10.8, which concludes the *theôria* discussion, instead of continuing with a discussion of education in 10.9 and then turning to the concerns of the city in the *Politics*. *Theôria* should not destroy the city. In part, this is so for self-serving reasons—if it did, *theôria* would destroy the conditions for its own existence in human beings. Furthermore, for *theôria* to destroy the city would be to do something wrong.

Now, since we belong to the city, we are sometimes called upon to maintain its existence or to make it provide a better life, and this is a reasonable call, which we should not ignore even if we happen to be theorizing at the time. Furthermore, our responsibilities are not only to the city as a whole. By being in the city, we acquire responsibilities and duties, which must be respected and fulfilled if we are to live a good life. (And it is this, I will argue, that the unethical theoretician does not recognize.) We have responsibilities because of who we are and because of who we are related to by blood, friendship, or shared citizenship. Other people's claims upon the philosopher are no less fundamental than his claims on himself. Consequently, their claims are not deleted or silenced by the call of the theoretical. We have to take the good of others as an end in itself, which we should pursue. The good of others is not just important because it is instrumental to the philosopher's happiness; other people are important and have a claim on him on their own.[15] Aristotle's discussion of issues concerning the rotation of office in the *Politics* expresses this view:

> One might perhaps conceive that having authority over all [persons] is best, for in this way one would have authority over the greatest number and the noblest of actions. So [on this understanding] one who is capable of doing so should not leave those nearby to rule themselves but should deprive them of it, and a father should take no account of his children nor children of their father nor a friend for his friend nor take any thought for this: the best is what is most choiceworthy, and acting well is best. Perhaps, they argue truly in this if the most choiceworthy of existing things will be available to those who plunder and use force. But perhaps it is impossible that it be available, and this presupposition of theirs is false. For actions can no longer be noble for one who does not differ as much [from those he rules] as husband differs from wife, father from children, or master from slaves. So the transgressor could never make up later for the deviation from virtue he has already committed. Among similar persons nobility and justice are found in [ruling and being ruled] in turn, for this is something equal and similar. (*Pol.* 1325a34–b8)[16]

The needs of our fellow citizens must be taken into account.[17] We are not justified in trying to rule more in order to get more good for ourselves. On the contrary, I should give up office when my time is up, even if governing is the best life available to me, simply because others deserve it as much as I do. By the same token, we are not justified in shirking our responsibility to help rule, even if we would prefer to lead a theoretical life.

Sometimes, your community or your friends need your help and, many of those times, you should help them. The Aristotelian theoretician, then, recognizes the value of the good of the city and of the good of other citizens as goods in themselves. He is not choosing to act ethically only to stay out of trouble or only to make sure he has food and other necessities. He chooses to act ethically because he knows that being a human being living in a city, he has responsibilities that he must fulfill. If somebody happens to be born a god or beast among men, he is free to leave the city and to sever those ties, abandoning those responsibilities. However, the rest of us will not be able to do that, and we ought not. Sherman puts the point well:

> There are constraints on how contemplative activity must be pursued: not as a god would, but as a human would, within the boundaries defined by our social and moral lives. To pursue contemplation "as far as possible" means as far as the circumstances of practical action allow. Thus, contemplative reason might be what is most authoritative and best in a human being (1178a1–3), but it is neither, in virtue of that, the *only* human end, everything else subserving to it, nor (what, practically speaking, comes to much the same) the end, among other final ends, that always has pre-emptive status. (1989, 101)

The fine and noble remain in force. Ethical responsibilities remain crucial because we are and remain human beings living with others. Ethics is not just a means to *eudaimonia* which can be discarded if we find another, better, means. Rather, it involves an actual and true recognition of what one must do.[18] Ethically virtuous activity is more than a means. It is important in its own right as an integral part of the human function. If we focus on the higher part exclusively, we are pretending that we lack the lower part, and we are misconstruing our end.

If the philosopher is lucky, there is no need for her to help rule the city because there are other capable individuals who want to rule and who are going to be good at it, and then she can in good conscience devote her life to studying the world. Circumstances will permit this lucky philosopher to spend as much time as humanly possible studying. If her luck holds, she will be doing this with an adequate but not excessive supply of external resources, in the company of real friends. Whatever calls the fine makes upon her will take place during the necessary downtime from *theôria*—because she is still human and not a god, she cannot study all the time. However, circumstances usually do not cooperate that nicely. Sometimes, and perhaps often, the requirements of the fine conflict with theoretical activity, both when we choose a way of life and when we make decisions about what to do now. Circumstances might require that every man do his duty; the good of the city might require the woman to rule because the other candidates are less well suited or because justice requires that she take her turn. Those who manage to escape a public career will still be faced with situations where friends need help and family members face crises when they prefer to theorize. Study can wait—friends and cities in need cannot. The nature of Aristotelian study is such that it is never in immediate crisis because it is not for the sake of anything else and does not have results. We can always come back to it, take up where we left off, after we have dealt with more time-sensitive matters.

Conflict between the ethical and the contemplative seems to occur in two types of situations: First, it arises when I ask myself how I should live (to which activity I should give primacy): I have inherited the throne or I live in a democracy where I am expected to help rule, but I would prefer to live a life of *theôria*. This is the famous Greek question of whether philosophy or politics is the best life to choose, the dispute which Aristotle mentions in the *Politics* (and which I quoted earlier). Should I devote my life to making my city as good as possible, or should I become a philosopher? Second, conflict arises when I ask which activity I should pursue and exercise in a given situation: My father needs my help right now, but I want to study. Aristotle would respond to the first question by saying that those who have the ability and who are free to pursue a life of *theôria* should do so. In some situations, however, the city demands a sacrifice of the individual, or he lacks freedom for some other reason, and he must help to rule instead of theorizing. When I am free to do so, I should study. However, even if I have been lucky enough to be able to choose a life of study, I am not excused from ethical obligations. In some situations, like the second scenario above, ethics makes demands upon me that it would be foul for me to refuse, and I must meet them. *Theôria* requires liberty and thus is the right choice only if I indeed am free from conflicting strong responsibilities.

But I will not be. To have a life where the fine never made demands on me would be to have an inhuman life, either bestial and divine. Since I am neither beast nor god, such a life would be either too high or too low for me. A human being with the capacity for *theôria* cannot and should not live the type of life where the conflict between the fine and *theôria* doesn't exist. To avoid the conflict by giving up *theôria* would be to diminish oneself. To avoid it by transcending ethics would be possible only by leaving the city, and that is possible only for a beast or a god. As long as we remain human beings, we *are* that conflict, that tension. Human nature is divided; the question of the best life for us cannot be given a simple answer.[19]

THE UNETHICAL THEORETICIAN

If the theoretician has been properly habituated, he will recognize that the ethical must play a crucial role. But as I mentioned earlier, he may not have been habituated properly. He may have started doing *theôria* without being properly habituated first, and thus may never have learned to recognize the force of the fine. What will we say to and about such a man? It will have to be something like this: By ignoring ethics and the city, the unethical theoretician is forgetting that he is a human being. He is trying to live a life that is denying vital aspects of his nature and his crucial responsibilities to the city. He does not see things the way the *phronimos* sees them, and this means that he does not see rightly. The unethical theoretician fails to recognize that the best life altogether is not the best life for beings like him. He is pretending that he can live a life where the requirements of the fine simply are absent, and thus never threaten one's studying. If he were able to do that—if he could in fact live a theoretical life in which ethical issues never arose—Aristotle would not fault him for leaving human things behind.

If a man truly became divine, it would be right for him to leave ethics and other human things behind. But Aristotle does not believe that human beings can become gods. And neither does the unethical theoretician. He is not willing to live without a human society. Instead, he continues to live among us, taking advantage of others' ethical behavior, which maintains the good of the city. He is right to notice that ethics belongs to the unavoidably human aspects of our existence and that, if we were gods, we would not need it. However, he fails to recognize that as long as we remain human beings, it is a necessary part of the good life for us.

Trying to persuade the unethical theoretician of the error of his ways, Aristotle could try to argue that a lack of ethical virtue will impair the exercise of intellectual virtue. In Williams's words, he might try to "represent the bad person as a compulsive addict, an unenviable wreck" (1985, 44). Aristotle seems to gesture in this direction when he argues that base people's souls experience serious internal conflict, that they do not dare to be by themselves, and that they are utterly miserable (1166b6–28). In such a state, presumably, engaging in *theôria* would become virtually impossible. However, that line of reasoning does not strike me as very promising because I see no reason to assume that the bad person must be like that. At best, it reestablishes that he cannot completely neglect the virtues—insofar as he is rational, he must recognize their instrumental role. (I will discuss this further in the next chapter.) Furthermore, Aristotle usually recognizes that bad people can function quite effectively (as Williams also notes). Most importantly, he sees that they can be clever and thus can reason to get to their chosen ends. Indeed, Book 7 gives a very different portrait of the bad man. The intemperate man seems quite harmonious; his desires and reason point him in the same (bad) direction. Unlike the incontinent person who is at war with himself, despising his bad desires, the intemperate man is perfectly content with himself.

In responding to the unethical theoretician, Aristotle can say everything I have just said and more, but the problem remains—the other does not see the situation as Aristotle does because he has not been habituated properly. From within ethics, it is clear that he is neglecting something crucial—but it is equally clear that he will not be forced to admit it. Consequently, the Kantian objection rings true. Aristotle seems to make ethics optional rather than mandatory because instead of a categorical imperative ("be ethical!"), he provides only a hypothetical imperative ("If you want to be happy, be ethical"). And this imperative does not persuade the bad theoretician that he should be ethical because he knows that ethics is not the only or even the best route to happiness; *theôria* provides a different and superior route. Thus, the theoretician revises the imperative: "If you want to be happy, be ethical *or theoretical*"; he chooses to be theoretical; and he reasonably concludes that he does not need to be ethical. Aristotle would have to say that the theoretician would not know what he is missing but would be missing it nevertheless, and in that respect he would be in the same boat as the person whose habits incline him towards appreciation of a life of pleasure or honor. His mistake is the same as that of a person who pursues a life of pleasure—he forgets that he is human. But while the pleasure seeker takes himself for an animal, the unethical theoretician takes himself for a god.

If Aristotle were trying to defend ethics by arguing that it is necessary for *eudaimonia*, the possibility of a happy but unethical theoretician would be a serious threat to his argument. Happiness would be the goal, ethics the means, and the unethical theoretician would have found a different and superior means to that end, thus making ethics optional. However, I will argue in the remaining chapters, Aristotle is not trying to defend ethics by suggesting that it is a means to the human end. Rather, he regards ethical virtue as part of the human end, agreeing with Kant that we must aim at the ethical for its own sake. Ethical virtue is not a mere instrumental good. As I will show, this means that the bad man cannot find an alternative path to the end, but it also means that he is not aiming at this end in the first place, so that his failure to reach it will not matter to him. In the next chapter, I will examine Aristotle's Book 1 argument which argues that true happiness requires ethical virtue, showing that even though it is a powerful argument, it will not persuade the bad man that he ought to be ethical.

chapter four

THE ARGUMENT
OF THE *ETHICS*

Discerning and Reaching the Highest End

Aristotle's argument in Book 1 of the *Ethics* shows what role ethics plays in the good life. Might this argument influence the skeptic and the bad man? As previously noted, Aristotle is sometimes thought to be trying to sway them by showing that the virtues are necessary means to happiness. I have noted that if he does this, the unethical theoretician poses a serious threat to his argument. However, I have also suggested that Aristotle views ethics as part of *eudaimonia*, not as a mere instrument. Consequently, he should not be trying to argue for ethics by showing that it is a means to happiness. So what is his argument and against whom will it be effective? This chapter will examine Aristotle's argument for the ethical life in the *Ethics*, asking what it proves with regards to ethics and how persuasive it is. In particular, can it persuade the bad person?

I will first examine the relevant part of *Ethics* 1.1–7, up to but not including the function argument. I will argue that Aristotle starts from the fundamental rationality and teleological structure of human action. He argues that our ends are hierarchically ordered (the highest are pursued for their own sake, the lowest are pursued for the sake of something else, and, in between, some are pursued for both reasons) and then spells out what that implies regarding how one must act. He argues that *eudaimonia* is our highest end and shows why *eudaimonia* cannot be honor, virtue, or pleasure. I will, in general, defend his argument up to this point as plausible and powerful, suggesting that it should persuade any rational person. However, it does not in itself generate an ethics. Knowing that there is a highest *telos* called *eudaimonia* does not yet yield specific advice for how we should act. First, we need to know the content of the end and what means might promote it. The question, then, is whether Aristotle can show that *eudaimonia* has a specific content, that it is more than just a shorthand label for "whatever I want."

The function argument is intended to do just that by showing that *eudaimonia* is excellent rational activity (activity in accordance with *aretê*). I will defend Aristotle's claim that we have a function (*ergon*) and argue that it is very plausible to say that our function is rational activity done excellently. However, I will suggest that the bad man need not accept that it is his end to perform the human function. Furthermore, the function argument does not give us an ethics either; we need to know why we should believe that the virtues will help us perform our function. In other words, why should we regard them as the relevant excellences? In considering the role of the virtues, I will argue that while Aristotle establishes the importance for intellectual virtues and an instrumental need for the ethical virtues (i.e., the virtues of character), his argument falls short in two ways. First, it does not show why good functioning requires that we give ethical virtues an intrinsic value. Consequently, the argument will not persuade the bad theoretician who can argue that he will reach the human end by focusing on excellence in *theôria* and thus does not need ethical virtues. Second, Aristotle is not able to show that a rational person must view excellent performance of the human function as her highest end. This means that, just as Kant feared, the bad person can dismiss Aristotle's argument as hypothetical, accepting that it provides a path to the human end but denying that she herself has any interest in reaching the human end.

THE GOOD AS *TELOS*, AND TELEOLOGICAL ACTION (1.1)

Aristotle begins the *Ethics* by stating that every action and every decision (as well as every craft and every investigation) seems to aim at some good, and he approvingly cites the description of the good as "what everything seeks."[1] In other words, our pursuits are teleological (intentional); in them, we are always aiming for something.[2] As Nussbaum puts it, "humans and other animals move about from place to place because there are things that they want or need and things that they see or think that bear on how they are to get them" (1986, 267). The connection between desire and goal is logical because we cannot give an account of the desire without mentioning the goal, and it is causal because the goals are what makes things happen (ibid, 268). If we did not want anything, we would not move. The teleological structure of human pursuits can be clearly seen in Aristotle's account of decision (*prohairesis*) in 6.2. Actions and the other human pursuits identified in the beginning of 1.1 are based on decisions. Thus, they are (or should be) goal-oriented activities in accordance with reason. This means that human pursuits are different from random behavior because they are teleological, issuing from a decision that in turn issues from a desire for an end and from having reasoned about how to achieve that end. While Aristotle does not say so here, the *Ethics* later makes clear that such behavior is specifically human (i.e., it is different from the behavior of other animals).

When we act, we can and do aim for many different kinds of goals, but Aristotle suggests that we are always aiming for some good. This sounds like a controversial claim, but I do not think Aristotle means it to be. He does not mean that we always aim for something that really is good (for us or for any-body else). Rather, we aim at what we deem good and, I think, he takes "what I deem good" to simply refer to "whatever I want." In other words, Aristotle's point is that if we aim for something, it is because we want it; it is an end we want to achieve. If we build a boat, we do so because we believe that the end of building (i.e., a boat) is in some sense good. We might believe it to be good for many different reasons; we might think that the boat is use-ful or beautiful, that it will impress our neighbors, or that we will get paid for building it. Starting with the function argument, Aristotle will argue that it is possible (and that it often happens) that our end really is not good, that we must distinguish between the end people in fact aim at and their true end, which they should aim at. People can misidentify the good, assuming things good that really are not, or not recognizing what is good when they see it. Thus, (part of) the task of ethics will be to help us identify what is good, what should be an end for us, and how to reach it.

However, in 1.1 and 1.2, Aristotle argues that we can figure out what end we should aim at by recognizing that the many existing ends can be ordered hierarchically. We need not use a distinction between good and bad ends. The guiding principle for the ordering is what is done for the sake of what. The higher ends, Aristotle explains, "are more choiceworthy than all the ends subordinate to them since the lower ends are also pursued for the sake of the higher" (1094a15–16). Thus, we get a threefold division, of increasing value and importance:

1. Pursued for the sake of something else
2. Pursued for the sake of something else and for its own sake
3. Pursued for its own sake and not for the sake of anything else

This threefold division will be crucial for Aristotle's argument in the *Ethics*. Later in Book 1, Aristotle will of course argue that only *eudaimonia* belongs to the third category, and that it is thus the highest end. He locates pleasure, virtue, and honor in the second category, which indicates that they are inferior to *eudaimonia*. Wealth belongs in the first category and is thus inferior to pleasure, virtue, and honor.

Aristotle has been accused of using the claim that that all action is teleological to infer that there must be a highest *telos* at which all actions aim. That is a fallacy analogous to the one involved in saying that because all roads lead somewhere; they must all lead to the same place. However, as numerous recent commentators have noted, there seems to be no reason to assume that Aristotle's reasoning commits this fallacy or that he believes himself to have established the existence of a highest good in 1.1. Rather, 1.1 seems to proceed on a conceptual level, asking what we mean by a "highest end." Aristotle has merely begun his discussion of the highest end, arguing that it must be pursued for its own sake and not for the sake of something else. He has not yet tried to show that there is a highest *telos* so, at this point in the discussion, it is still possible that nothing is pursued only for its own sake, that is, that the third category is empty. Furthermore, he has not yet argued for his view that there is only one highest end rather than a number of different highest ends. (Kant, for example, argues that ethics is an end that is and should be completely separate from the end of being happy but that each is desirable for its own sake and not for the sake of something else.) Both these options need to be eliminated.

WHY EVERYTHING CANNOT BE DONE FOR THE SAKE OF SOMETHING ELSE (1.2)

In 1.2, Aristotle explores and rejects the possibility that everything is done simply for the sake of something else:

Suppose, then, that the things achievable by action have some end that we wish for because of itself, and because of which we wish for the other things, and that we do not choose everything because of something else—for if we do, it will go on without limit [*eis apeiron*], so that desire will prove to be empty and futile. Clearly, this end will be the good, that is to say, the best good. (1094a18–23)

The final sentence suggests that this argument has shown that there is exactly one highest end, excluding both the possibility that there is no highest end and the possibility that there is more than one such end. If Aristotle takes himself to have shown both, he seems to be mistaken. However, in the beginning of 1.7, Aristotle treats the possibility of more than one highest end as still open: "If there is some end of everything achievable in action, the good achievable in action will be this end; if there are more ends than one, [the good achievable in action] will be these ends" (1097a22–23). The final sentence here in 1.2 claims more than Aristotle should and needs to at this point. The work of 1.2 is to establish that there is at least one highest end, nothing more.

But even that might seem to be quite an ambitious project. Exactly what is the argument for the existence of at least one highest end? It is a *reductio*, and the unacceptable conclusion is that our desire is empty and futile. To avoid having to draw that conclusion, we must assume that there must be some end which we want for its own sake and for the sake of which we want other things. But is that conclusion of futility really impossible? Might one not just dismiss Aristotle's insistence that desire must not be futile as wishful thinking? Why should not desires be futile; why should life make sense?

In stating his argument, Aristotle says that unless there is something that we desire for its own sake, the result will be that the chain of our desires goes on without limit. So what does this mean? Aristotle's point seems to be that if we did not want some things for their own sake, our desires would hang in the air, as it were, and we would not know what to do. According to Aristotle, desires constitute reasons for acting (though not necessarily good reasons).[3] But if there were nothing that we desired for its own sake, some of our desires would form a regression towards an infinitely distant point, a for b, b for c, c for d, and so on. Other desires would form circles, and we would want a for b, b for c, c for d, and d for a. The result in either case is the same: The chain does not end; the explanation for one desire is explained by reference to another and so on ad infinitum and hence they are not explained at all. We would be left without any reason to act because there would be nothing we really wanted.

Another way of expressing Aristotle's point is by saying that if we are going to act, there must be ends which we really want to attain, highest ends. We cannot pursue everything because we think it can serve as a means to something else. It is the end that gives meaning to the pursuit of the means. Without an end in mind, the pursuit of means is meaningless. If action is to be rational, there must be ends that we strive for and means that we use to attain those ends. In other words, the activity must be teleological. But that is not all. To be rational, an activity must ultimately aim at one of the highest ends, rather than at lower ends, because the lower ends are for the sake of the higher. It is irrational to aim for a lower end at the expense of a higher end and to pursue a means as if it were an end. (This will play a crucial role later on in Aristotle's argument.) An action is truly in accordance with reason only if it aims at the highest end or at a lower end as a means to the highest end. That is, an action is not rational simply because it will get you to your stated end. It is rational only if it (attempts) to get you to(wards) the highest end.

If we were to assume that there are means but no ends and that our desires form circular chains or infinite regresses, we would place ourselves in the same situation as those who deny the principle of contradiction. We would have to accept that all alternatives are equally good (or bad) and hence would have no reason to act:

> It is most evident that no one of those who posit this doctrine [of denying noncontradiction], or anyone else, is disposed in his actions in the same way. For why does a man walk to Megara and not stay where he is with the thought that he is walking to Megara? And why does he not walk straight into a well or over a precipice, if such happens to be in his way, but appear to guard himself against it, with the thought that it is not equally good and not good to fall in? Clearly, then, he believes one course of action to be better and the opposite not better. (*Met.* 1008b12–19)

As Aristotle's argument in the *Metaphysics* shows, it would be difficult or impossible for those who refuse to accept that some actions are better than others to live by their words.

Furthermore, on the Aristotelian picture of things, "thought by itself moves nothing" (1139a36), so desire must help drive action. Then, trying to argue for (or even express) the conclusion that all desire is empty and futile involves self-contradiction. This is so because it requires us to argue that rational action is impossible, even though argument is a form of rational action. Thus, our argument could only be successful if such action were possible. However, if the argument were successful, it would prove that rational action is impossible and if that were so, the argument could not be successful. Of course, if we were irrational creatures, incapable of rational activity, such self-contradiction would be just what would be expected. The hypothesis that we are irrational without knowing it cannot be eliminated logically, at least not by us. However, while we cannot prove the possibility of rational action, it is a necessary assumption. If we are going to try to act, we need to maintain meaningful distinctions between action and mere behavior, between rationality and irrationality. If we are going to be creatures who engage in argument making, we need to assume that at least some of our actions are rational. That is, we must believe that they are and can be directed towards some goal that we want to achieve for its own sake, not just for the sake of something else (on pains of infinite regress). (I also suspect that Aristotle would have very little sympathy for the suggestion that we might all be irrational without knowing it.) If people reject the possibility of rational action, they thereby place themselves outside the realm of reason. They no longer believe it possible to argue rationally; there will be no point in arguing with them, and this relieves the rest of us from the task of trying to persuade them that they are mistaken—one might as well argue with vegetables.

Finally, it is tempting but, I think, futile, to try to expand this argument for the existence of at least one highest end in order to show that there must be exactly one highest end. Rational argument requires thinking that it sometimes is possible to act rationally, not that it always is possible. From the requirement that actions in general be rational, it does not follow that every action can and always has to be rational. At this point of the argument, at least, it remains possible that there are, say, five highest ends and that there are no grounds for giving one priority over the other. In some situations, then, we really might be in the situation of Buridan's ass, forced to make a choice without any reason to go either way. In other situations, we are in the situation of Sophocles' Antigone, forced to bring about disastrous consequences no matter what we choose. (I do not mean to say that Aristotle thought this to be possible—I am merely suggesting that he has not yet shown why it is not.)

So far, Aristotle's argument shows that, as rational creatures, we must accept that there is at least one highest end, an end that we want for its own sake and not as a means to something else. Once we accept the existence of such an end, the ability to reach it becomes central. The existence of a highest end implies a set of directives as to how we ought to act: Our actions should be aiming at that end; we must not pursue other, lower ends at the expense of higher ends. Almost certainly, if there is a goal, some ways of getting there work whereas others do not, and some work better than others. It would be irrational to pursue other things instead of the highest end. It would be irrational in a very basic way; the highest *telos* would be what we really want but we would still be acting in a way that did not enable us to approach it.

For the same reason, the rational agent will need to consider his life as a whole when he makes decisions about how to act, asking how a given action will affect his life and whether or not it will promote his highest end. Aristotle writes:

> [Since we have established that] everybody able to live according to his own purposive choice [*prohairesin*] should set before him some object for noble [*kalôs*] living to aim at—either honor or else glory or wealth or culture [*paideian*]—on which he will keep his eyes fixed in all his conduct (since clearly it is a mark of much folly not to have one's life regulated with regard to some End), it is therefore most necessary first to decide within oneself, neither hastily nor carelessly, in which of the things that belong to us the good life consists, and what are the indispensable conditions for men's possessing it. (*EE* 1214b6–12)

The need for a highest end that organizes our goals and activities is independent of the need for ethics; we need it even if we decide that wealth is the highest end. If a person lives according to choice (*prohairesis*), it is not enough for him to consider the now when making decisions about what to do; he must also consider the future or he could end up sacrificing more important ends for the sake of less important ones. He will probably not chase after a lower end now if he would have to do so at the expense of a higher end later. Consequently, he needs enough self-control to be able to postpone the satisfaction of current desires when necessary, and it will be desirable for him to be able to control and modify desires that seem to interfere with his ability to reach the highest end. Finally, in order to increase his chances of reaching his highest end (and as many of the lower ends as possible in addition), he will need to engage in reflection. At the very least, he will have to decide what his different ends are, how they relate to each other, whether there are tensions between different ends (and, if so, which one to prioritize), and the means to these various ends.

We have, then, a *very* sketchy code of action; the beginning of an ethics, but one that is little more than the bare bones of the structure of rational action. So far, we know very little about what the *telos* is like, so we do not know what we need to do in order to reach it, that is, which actions get us closer and which actions remove us. It still seems possible that the *telos* is relative to the individual's desires and wishes, that it is best glossed as "whatever I want most of all" (a conative conception of the good or end). If that is so, the existence of a *telos* for each person will not help us in the project of arguing for an ethics. Aristotle has to shift from a conative to a normative *telos*, from "whatever I want" to "what I ought to aim at," and, of course, he needs to provide an argument for that transition.[4] At this point, it still seems possible that the required code of behavior is different for each individual or group of individuals and that at least some of these codes are immoral and self-serving. Aristotle needs to establish a link between the highest *telos* and ethical behavior and show that the required behavior is not different for each individual. In order to bridge these gaps, Aristotle now goes on to argue that there is only one *telos*, that it is determined by our nature, and that reaching it requires virtuous action (indeed, he will argue that rational virtuous activity *is* the *telos*). After an aside on method (1.3), he starts by investigating the nature of the highest end.

THE SINGLE HIGHEST END: *EUDAIMONIA* (1.4–5)

In 1.4, Aristotle introduces the word *eudaimonia,* saying that people agree that happiness is good and the highest end. By making that identification, however, he notes that he has merely exchanged one name for another—"good" for "happiness"—because there is little agreement about what happiness is. People already rightly believe that their end is happiness, but ordinary conceptions about what happiness really is are mistaken. Aristotle then eliminates possible candidates for the title of the highest good by using two different sets of criteria, both of which are conceptual: First, the identity of happiness and the highest end enables Aristotle to transfer the criterion for what can count as a highest end to what can count as happiness. In other words, happiness must be something that can be pursued for its own sake, and everything else is or should be pursued for the sake of happiness. Thus, what people (especially now) may have taken to be a subjective question of happiness—What do I want? What do I like?—becomes an objective question about what candidate for the title of happiness can serve as a final end. But this is just a small step. So far, it is possible that many different answers meet these criteria and that they might still make essential reference to my idiosyncratic desires.

Second, Aristotle introduces other conceptual restrictions on what might count as *eudaimonia*, arguing that it must be "something of our own and hard to take from us" (1095b27) and that it cannot involve suffering the "worst evils and misfortunes" (1096a1). In 1.5, Aristotle discusses honor, wealth, virtue, and pleasure, and concludes that none of them can be the highest end. The exclusion of virtue should be startling at first, especially to those of us who know virtue will have a crucial role in *eudaimonia*. Aristotle denies that *eudaimonia* is virtue, which still allows him to affirm that *eudaimonia* is virtuous activity. His point in saying that *eudaimonia* is not virtue, then, is simply that *eudaimonia* is not just about what I am but also about what I do; my virtue must be realized in activity. The exclusion of honor and wealth are easier to grasp. Aristotle argues that honor is not really what we want. We would like to be honored not for just anything, but rather because of our virtue. This means that we recognize virtue as a higher end. Honor is also problematic because it is not up to us; we are honored by others, so if honor were the highest end, our happiness would depend upon other people. Thus, it would not be something of our own and difficult to take away from us. Wealth cannot be the highest end because it is a means, choiceworthy for the sake of some end but not valuable in itself.[5]

Finally, Aristotle dismisses the life of pleasure seeking rather abruptly, claiming that it is slavish and undignified. Why? It seems to me that, given his criteria (which I consider reasonable), pleasure has a good case: We enjoy pleasure for its own sake; can it meaningfully be said to be enjoyed for the sake of anything else? It will be absent in a life where we are hounded by great evils. Aristotle's reasons for dismissing pleasure are made clear only in 10.2–5 where he discusses pleasure at some length. He acknowledges that there is an intimate relation between pleasure and happiness, but he argues that pleasure abstracted from the activities from which we derive it cannot be happiness. His central argument against pleasure as the highest good is that we distinguish between what more or less discriminating people take pleasure in, saying that whereas some pleasures are good and correct, others are bad and incorrect. The possibility of there being correct and incorrect pleasures shows that pleasure is not the highest end. There must be something higher that we use as a standard in judging pleasures.

In 1.7, Aristotle turns to the task of showing that there is a single highest end. He reiterates the already familiar point that different actions and crafts have different ends. The end of all of them, if such an end exists, would be the one "for the sake of which the other things are done" (1097a19). Each science has one such end: in medicine, it is health; in generalship, victory, and so on. So is there "some end of everything achievable in action," an end over and above health and victory? If so, it will be the good, and it will be the only highest end because it would be the end of everything (by definition). That end must belong to the third category; that is, it must be wanted for its own sake and not for the sake of anything else. In other words, Aristotle says, such an end must be complete without qualification; it must be "always choiceworthy in its own right" (1097a34). It must also be self-sufficient, something that "all by itself . . . makes a life choiceworthy and lacking nothing" (1097b15).

Does anything fit these requirements? Aristotle argues that happiness more than anything else is complete without qualification; only it is placed in the third category. He seems to reach this conclusion by examining other possible candidates, eliminating those that cannot fulfill the formal requirements. In the field of candidates that Aristotle considers, he thinks the superiority of *eudaimonia* is clear. Other desirable things—honor, pleasure, understanding, virtue—fall into the second category.[6] That is, they are complete and choiceworthy because they are wanted for their own sake. However, they are not unconditionally complete and choiceworthy because they are also wanted for the sake of happiness. Happiness, on the other hand, is wanted for itself, but it is never wanted for the sake of anything else. In other words, happiness is the only thing we want which cannot serve as a means for something else that we want. Finally, unlike the other candidates, happiness is self-sufficient. In other words, once we have happiness, we do not want anything else: "We posit the self-sufficient to be that which taken by itself makes one's way of life worthy of choice and lacking in nothing" (1097b15). This means that happiness is the highest end, alone in the third category. The onus is now on the opponent—can he come up with either something that we want but not because it promotes happiness or something for the sake of which we want happiness?[7]

THE FUNCTION ARGUMENT

Aristotle has argued that there is exactly one highest end—*eudaimonia*. But what is *eudaimonia*? Can Aristotle show that it has a determinate content or is *eudaimonia* just a placeholder? So far, we have learned that it must be unconditionally complete, choiceworthy for its own sake, and self-sufficient, and that it therefore is not money, honor, virtue, or pleasure. We also know that it probably is connected to honor, pleasure, and virtue because we pursue these goods thinking that in addition to being desirable in themselves, they also lead to *eudaimonia*. While happiness is not identical to honor, pleasure, or virtue it may include them or be otherwise connected to them. The notion of *eudaimonia*, however, remains sketchy, and Aristotle has not shown why we should believe that the highest end is the same for all of us. Aristotle thinks that we can gain clarity as well as normativity by considering the human function because "the good, i.e., [doing] well . . . for whatever has a function and [characteristic] action seems to depend on [lit., be in] its function [*en tô ergô dokei tagathon einai kai to eu*]" (1097b28). The function argument is to show that my essence determines my good, that what I am determines what I should aim at in order to be happy. Because I am what I am, I should do *x*. We are essentially rational agents, so the life of a rational agent is the happy life for us.

Until now, Aristotle has been concerned with drawing out the implications of saying that our actions always are goal oriented. He has stressed that their goal-oriented nature necessitates that we organize our activities by distinguishing between instrumental and intrinsically valuable activities. He has labeled the highest goal *eudaimonia* and argued that it alone is what we pursue for its own sake. But he has not yet explained its content. In the function argument, Aristotle gives *eudaimonia* content, and he introduces a normative rather than a conative view of happiness. In other words, he tries to show that *eudaimonia* is not just whatever we want. Rather, its content is determined by what kinds of beings we are and since we are all the same in kind, it is (more or less) the same for all of us. My ultimate goal has a definite content, which is independent of my whims and desires.

Aristotle's procedure for gaining understanding about *eudaimonia* by considering the human function raises a number of questions: Why should we believe that we have a function? What might that function be? Why would performing our function be our end? Do we really need the virtues in order to perform our function well? And, finally, does the function argument prove to each of us that we should adopt Aristotle's conception of happiness as our highest end? In answering these questions, I will suggest that Aristotle's argument shows why it is plausible to view rational activity as our function and to say that performing it well is our end. Aristotle also makes a good case that the intellectual virtues are essential to good functioning and that to function well we have at least a limited instrumental need for the ethical virtues. However, he does not establish that the ethical virtues are intrinsically valuable. Furthermore, while the function argument proves to some of us that we should adopt Aristotle's conception of happiness as our highest end, it does not prove it to all of us. The skeptic and the bad man will not be persuaded even if they are being quite rational. In the next chapter, I will argue that the failure of the argument at this point is unavoidable and that its failure illuminates the limitations of argument and reason.

What Is the Human Function?

What does it mean to say that human beings have an *ergon* (a characteristic activity or function)? The *ergon* of an eye is to see well. To reach its *telos*, the eye must perform that *ergon*—indeed, to perform its *ergon* well *is* its *telos*. But an eye does not just see, it also moves from left to right, its pupil expands, the eye becomes wet, and so on. However, these other activities do not constitute its *ergon*. They are only means to the end. Moving and other such activities are also shared with other things. In contrast, Aristotle argues, a characteristic activity needs to distinguish the actor from other kinds of actors, and it needs to be an activity that is essential to the actor. Is there some activity that belongs to human beings in the same way that seeing belongs to the eye? Searching for our *ergon*, Aristotle identifies three basic categories of activities for living beings: nutrition, reproduction, and growth; movement and sense perception; and "some sort of life of action of the [part of the soul] that has reason [*praktikê tis tou logon echontos*]" (1098a4). He excludes the first two categories from consideration, arguing that we do not perform our *ergon* when we eat or when we perceive something. Such activities are shared with other animals; they are not unique (*idion*) to us among living things. Rational activity, however, is not shared with other animals and Aristotle concludes that if there is a human function, it is "activity of the soul in accord with reason [*logon*] or requiring reason" (1098a7).

Now, what does Aristotle mean by saying that our function should be *idion*? We naturally interpret him as meaning that the function will be one that only human beings have. That is, each kind of being has something that only it can do and this will be its function. That cannot be what Aristotle means. If our function had to be unique in that strict sense, contemplation could not be part of the human function because, as Aristotle points out in Book 10, we share it with the gods. Rather, our function would have to be ethical reasoning and action. However, in Book 10, Aristotle clearly sees contemplation as primary and moral reasoning as only secondary happiness, so we must be performing our function at least as much when we contemplate as when we deliberate on ethical issues. This suggests that our *ergon* does not have to be unique to us. Aristotle is not trying to exclude activities that we have in common with any being; rather, he is interested in excluding activities we share with lower beings.[8] In the *Topics*, Aristotle distinguishes between two senses of *idion*, an absolute and a relative (102a18–28). A property is *idion* to human beings in an absolute sense if it cannot belong to other beings (Aristotle's example in the *Topics* is the capacity for learning grammar). But a property might also be *idion* in a relative sense. For example, Aristotle explains, when we say that being a biped is *idion* to man, we do not mean that only men are bipeds. Rather, we are saying that being a biped is *idion* to man in relation to a horse or a dog. In the same way, our function is *idion* to us not absolutely but relative to the other animals.

Once we learn that our *ergon* is activity in accordance with reason, the claim that we have an *ergon* should no longer seem odd. Furthermore, the thesis that our *ergon* is rational activity does not seem to depend on Aristotle's psychology and its three basic categories of activities of living things.[9]

Now, critics have suggested that Aristotle is wrong in saying that rational activity is the only unique human activity. Williams writes:

> If one approached without preconceptions the question of finding characteristics which differentiate men from other animals, one could as well, on these principles, end up with a morality which exhorted men to spend as much time as possible in making fire; or developing peculiarly human physical characteristics; or having sexual intercourse without regard to season; or despoiling the environment and upsetting the balance of nature; or killing things for fun. (1976, 59)

It seems to me that most of these examples of alternative activities fail to undermine the claim that rational activity is unique. Except for sexual intercourse out of season, all of them are instances of rational activities (they require reason), not alternatives to rational activities. However, sexual intercourse out of season does seem to identify an aspect of human beings that is unique—we are the only animals that reproduce year-round.[10] Furthermore, we can come up with additional examples. For example, the ability to laugh seems to be unique to human beings. Thus, Williams seems to be right in saying that the list of unique human characteristics includes more than just rational activity.

In order to counter Williams's objection, we need to recognize that Aristotle uses uniqueness among animals as a necessary but not a sufficient condition.[11] In addition to being unique, the human *ergon* must also be something that is special *and important* about us, something that makes us what we are. It must refer to our essence. In the *Topics*, Aristotle notes that *idion* is sometimes used to refer to the essence to a thing: "Part of the peculiarity [*idiou*] indicates the essence [*to ti ên einai*] and part does not do so" (101b19–21).[12] When he says that our function is *idion*, he seems to have this sense of *idion* in mind. In other words, Aristotle assumes—and I agree—that our rational ability is a more important distinguishing fact about us than our sexual practices because it permeates everything about us, everything we do.[13] If humanity lost the ability to reason and to act for the sake of reasons, that loss would make the species into something very different, something no longer human. How different would we be, as human beings, if we were sexually active only in the fall? Granted, we would be strange human beings, but I do not think anybody would argue that we would no longer be human.[14]

Why Does the Function Make Us Happy?

Given that rational activity is our function, why should we believe that engaging in our characteristic activity will make us happy? Aristotle seems to think that this is obvious, but I will suggest that it is not. Let us begin by trying to spell out his reasoning. There is a conceptual link between *ergon* and *telos*: To reach our end, we must perform our function. That is, performing our characteristic activity is what we have to do in order to reach our *telos*, or performing that activity is itself our *telos*. In the case of tools and crafts, this seems obvious: The purpose or end of a hammer is to achieve a state of affairs where nails have been driven into wood. The function of the hammer is to drive nails into wood. The characteristic activity of a boat builder aims to produce a boat (*telos*), and the activity (*ergon*) is boat building. The function of an eye is to see, and performing that function is also to attain its *telos*—seeing. In all of these cases, performing the *ergon* well is the way to the *telos*. In an analogous fashion, Aristotle argues, the characteristic human activity enables us to reach the human end. But *eudaimonia* is like seeing, not like boat building. While *eudaimonia* and seeing are both types of *praxis* (doing), boat building is a *poiêsis* (making).[15] A *poiêsis* generally has a product that is separate from the activity (the boat is not identical to the boat-building). This means that as long as the boat turns out well, it does not matter in what manner it is built. The boat building is a simple means to the end, i.e., the boat. In *eudaimonia*, in contrast, the end and the activity coincide. Performing the characteristic human activity is not a simple means to happiness. Rather, Aristotle argues, *eudaimonia* simply *is* performing our function well. To perform the human function well *is* to be happy, just as performing the eye's function well *is* to see well. (I will discuss that "well" later.) For Aristotle, reaching one's *telos* and developing one's nature fully—truly becoming what one is—are one and the same thing. Everything that can act expresses its nature in its function and reaches its end by engaging in that activity, just as one might say that a flutist expresses her nature and reaches her end as a musician by playing the flute, and playing it well. As human beings, we do not fully become ourselves, we are not fulfilled, unless we engage in rational activity.

These requirements cannot be fulfilled by arguing that reason certainly is useful and even crucial, but that nonetheless it is instrumental and properly put in the service of other ends. This would be confusing higher and lower ends. Rational activity is itself our *telos*, and it makes no sense to say that it is a means to a higher *telos*—there is no higher *telos*. (I will return to the issue of reason as instrumental.)

Now, it seems to me that a significant problem remains. We can accept Aristotle's argument that performing my function well is to complete my nature and to attain the human end. But the next step—saying that this is what happiness is, that this is what I really aim at—except that I do not know it—remains to be explained. Why should I accept that completing my nature will make me happy and that it should be my end? Why must the human end be my end? Why should I think that attaining normative happiness is the only or even the best way to attain conative happiness? If I do not believe that it is, why should I abandon my goal of conative happiness in order to attain normative happiness? Why should I accept rational activity as my end instead of viewing rational activity as merely instrumental? This difficulty, as it turns out, will reemerge in Aristotle's attempts to link ethical virtue and *phronêsis* to the human function and end, which is where I will turn now.

THE LINK TO VIRTUE (*ARETÊ*)

Saying that performing the human function is *eudaimonia* is not enough. Playing the harp creates music. However, it is not enough to play; we need to be able to play well, or we will end up making mere noise, not music. In order to play well, we need expertise and skill. We do not reach the *telos* by taking a crack at the *ergon*—we need to perform it well. Aristotle suggests that the same holds about performing the human function: in order to be happy, we need to perform the human function well. The goal is not just blundering away at living but to live well, not just performing the human function but to perform it well. Only thus does one reach the *telos*. That is, one needs skill at living in order to be *eudaimôn*.[16] One needs *aretê*.

Aristotle explains that a hammer has *aretê* if it is good at performing the function of a hammer, and a human being has *aretê* if she is good at performing the human function. In general, a virtue is a quality that helps *x* to perform its function well. That is, there is a conceptual connection between *ergon* and *aretê*. Aristotle explains the connection as follows:

> Every virtue causes its possessors to be in a good state and to perform their functions well. The virtue of eyes, for instance, makes the eyes and their functioning excellent, because it makes us see well; and similarly, the virtue of a horse makes the horse excellent, and thereby good at galloping, at carrying its riders, and at standing steady in the face of the enemy. If this is true in every case, the virtue of a human being will likewise be the state that makes a human being good and makes him perform his function well. (1106a17–24)

Given the connection already discussed between *ergon* and *telos* (i.e., in *poiêsis*, we get to the *telos* by performing the *ergon*; in *praxis*, that *telos* is doing the *ergon*), this means that *aretê* is a quality that enables *x* to reach its *telos*. We might call it skill at living—being able to reach the *telos* or, better, being able to participate in the activities that themselves are the *telos*. But what does skill at living have to do with the intellectual and ethical virtues that Aristotle analyzes in the *Ethics*?[17] Can the function argument show that being (morally) good is part of the human function? The argument needs to make the transition from being excellent at living to having the ethical virtues.

It is easy to understand how the purely intellectual virtues aid in performing the human function, given that Aristotle has concluded that the human function is "activity of the soul in accord with reason or requiring reason (1098a7). Surely, to exercise intellectual virtues simply *is* such activity. When I am engaged in *epistêmê*, for example, I am engaging in an activity that is in accord with reason and which also requires reason. Consequently, somebody who lacks intellectual virtue would not be able to perform the human function well, just as an item that lacks a sharp edge cannot cut and hence cannot perform the function of a knife well.

AN INSTRUMENTAL ROLE

What of the ethical virtues? Aristotle can make a solid case for a limited instrumental need for the executive ethical virtues (courage, temperance, and so on) by showing how a lack of certain ethical virtues disrupts teleological behavior.[18] Consequently, these virtues are needed if we are to perform our function well. Consider a coward for example. He might be a coward because he does not agree with Aristotle that courageous action should be part of his end. Instead, he believes that his own personal safety is paramount. In some situations, his cowardice will serve his perceived interests well; he will be safe, instead of risking his life. But his lack of courage is also likely to get in the way because his cowardly habits might make it impossible for him to act courageously even though he needs to do so in order to attain something that he wants. A coward is ruled by fear, and fear will sometimes overrule his better judgment about what would promote his perceived longer-term interests and about what risks might be worth taking.

If our actions are to express our intellectual commitment and our beliefs about what we should do, we need the relevant virtues. Otherwise, we would not have the strength of character we need actually to pursue the end we identify as the right one. Consequently, we would need to have been habituated properly, to the extent that we must have learned to keep our feelings and desires in check even in the face of danger or temptation. The nonrational part must agree with the rational part, thus enhancing or making rational activity possible. We need not accept the human end as our end to be persuaded by this argument, because some of the ethical virtues are needed to promote our ends in general, not just to promote the human end. A lack of virtues like courage is likely to disrupt the thoughtful pursuit of a merely conative end as well as the pursuit of *theôria*. Thus, it is in anybody's best interest to develop at least the executive virtues. Any rational person should upon reflection agree to at least this minimum need for virtues, recognizing that if he neglects the ethical virtues and develop bad habits, he might not be able to promote his chosen ends later. (He may of course fail to act based on this understanding.) For the same reason, he will need at least some practical reasoning—as I argued previously, he will need to be able to figure out how his different ends fit together and what actions promote each.

Now, this establishes only a limited role for the virtues and practical reason. If they are merely instrumental, it would be silly to pay too much attention to them. Instead, I should worry about them only as much as I need to;

I must not promote them at the expense of more important matters. They would not have value in themselves and could and should be sacrificed any time a higher end was at stake.

BEYOND INSTRUMENTALITY: LEARNING TO SEE

Of course, Aristotle believes that ethical virtue and *phronêsis* have a much more significant role. We should care about developing the virtues not just because they are useful but because they have intrinsic value and are part of the highest end. In short, they are worth promoting for their own sake: "[The virtues] we certainly choose because of themselves, since we would choose each of them even if it had no further result; but we also choose them for the sake of happiness" (1097b3–4). I am missing the point if I reduce ethics to the level of mere instrumentality, arguing that I should be courageous only when it promotes my other ends and that I otherwise need not worry about it. Virtue is not a mere means to the end; it is a part of the end (as is the activity of *phronêsis*). *Eudaimonia* is activity of the soul for the sake of the *kalon*. In order to attain *eudaimonia*, we must pursue the *kalon* for its own sake, because *eudaimonia* simply consists in a life of active pursuit of the *kalon* or, equivalently, a life of virtuous activity. To recognize the end is to realize that happiness is the activity of pursuing the fine.

What case can Aristotle make for saying that both ethical virtue and *phronêsis* are more than sometimes useful means to the end? Aristotle writes: "We fulfill our function insofar as we have *phronêsis* and virtue of character; for virtue makes the goal correct, and *phronêsis* makes the things promoting the goal [correct]" (1144a9–10). Virtue makes the end correct and *phronêsis* makes the means to that end correct. If that is so, *phronêsis* seems to deal simply with execution. To borrow Aristotle's archer image from 1.2, *phronêsis* handles the bow, figuring out how to shoot an arrow, how to tense the bow, when to release and so on. A *phronimos* can figure out how to get from point A to point B. At first glance, then, *phronêsis* seems to have the same obvious and noncontroversial link to the function as the purely intellectual virtues do. Through means/ends reasoning, it determines which actions are required to reach a given end. It orders ends, organizes our thoughts and actions, and it figures out what we should aim at and how to reach our end(s). Thus, it determines the means for getting to the end which we can see only because we are virtuous, and it involves understanding the whole hierarchy of ends, interrelations, how actions in one part affect the whole structure, and so on.

Without that sort of ability, our rational activity would indeed be hampered. We would be pursuing contradictory ends or acting in ways that remove us from our end instead of bringing us closer. We would not be able to get what we want.

If *phronêsis* merely made the means correct, it would be indistinguishable from cleverness. Yet the two are not the same: "*Phronêsis* is not cleverness, though it requires this capacity. [*Phronêsis,*] this eye of the soul, requires virtue in order to reach its fully developed state" (1144a29–30). Aristotle glosses cleverness as the ability "to do the actions that tend to promote whatever goal is assumed and to attain them" (1144a25). In contrast, *phronêsis* promotes the human end. The person with *phronêsis* can "deliberate finely about things that are good and beneficial for himself . . . about what sorts of things promote living well in general" (1140a26–28). If I were merely clever, I might be able to figure out what generosity requires, but I would not value generosity for its own sake, although I might recognize that seeming generous can be useful. Unlike *sophia* and *epistêmê*, then, *phronêsis* is not purely intellectual. Rather, it straddles the divide between the ethical and the intellectual.

Aristotle spells out the connection between virtue of character and *phronêsis* in the end of 6.13: "We cannot be fully good without *phronêsis*, or prudent without virtue of character" (1144b31–32). Without *phronêsis*, we could not figure out what to do to reach the end; without character virtue, we would not be able to see the end clearly (and thus would not have *phronêsis*, but at best cleverness). Moreover, character virtue requires *phronêsis*. Virtue without *phronêsis* is mere natural virtue; "full virtue cannot be acquired without *phronêsis*" (1144b17). *Phronêsis* requires virtue because the *phronimos* does not simply figure out what to do in order to attain end *x*. He also takes a further step, asking whether attaining end *x* will help or hinder the effort of attaining the human end. And, of course, he can do that only because he has a correct understanding of the human *telos*, which Aristotle says that the virtues provide. When we are talking about *phronêsis* in abstraction from ethical virtue, then, we are really only talking about cleverness. *Phronêsis* is inseparable from and impossible without the virtues.

As Irwin notes, the division of labor suggested by Aristotle's claim that virtue makes the end correct and *phronêsis* the means probably cannot be upheld:

> It is difficult to maintain, consistently with Aristotle's other remarks in [6.] 12–13, that virtue, quite independently of prudence [*phronêsis*], fixes the right end, and then prudence finds what promotes it. For

Aristotle has just insisted that virtue (which makes the end correct) requires prudence (which makes the things promoting the end correct); hence, it seems, we cannot make the end correct without making the things promoting the end correct. (1999, 255, §7)

Virtue and *phronêsis* are thoroughly interconnected and mutually dependent. You cannot have one without the other and if you could, each would fail to do its work in the absence of the other.

But how are we to understand the claim that the virtues (combined with *phronêsis*) enable us to see the highest end? When we learn in 1.4 that the human good is happiness and that everybody already knows this, discerning the end does not seem to be much of a problem. However, a couple of pages later, we learn that people's ideas of *eudaimonia* differ and that some of these ideas are wrong. We will not attain *eudaimonia* through having a lot of money, for example, even though many people believe that we can. Thus, the problem is not only learning to shoot an arrow. Many of us also aim in the wrong direction because we do not recognize the target. We might not understand that *eudaimonia* truly is normative *eudaimonia* and instead insist on pursuing other goals. A better analogy than target shooting (where it is obvious what you should be aiming at) would be hunting. In addition to knowing how to aim and fire, it is also necessary to learn how to recognize the target, being able to distinguish between a black bear and the neighbor's beloved Labrador retriever. And here, Aristotle states, the ethical virtues have a crucial role because they enable us to see the end better. Without the virtues, we cannot even recognize the target, so no matter how good we are at shooting, we still will not hit it. Mere cleverness, then, is worthless.

Without the virtues, we will not know what to aim for, so we will aim for the wrong things and consequently will not function rationally. In short, excellent rational activity requires the virtues because they make the end right (the bear and not the dog). Seeing the end correctly is part of rational activity, and without the virtues such seeing is impossible. Without the ethical virtues, I will not see that normative *eudaimonia* is my end. Only if we have both the virtues and *phronêsis* can our activity truly be rational; only then will we be fully rational. Rational activity requires *phronêsis* and not just cleverness because without *phronêsis*, we cannot see the whole picture. Or, equivalently, rational activity requires the virtues because without them, we cannot see the highest end; we will not recognize that normative *eudaimonia* is the highest end. Consequently, we will be pursuing conative rather than normative *eudaimonia*, hunting pets rather than bears.

When considered as a candidate for an argument for the role of the ethical virtues, this line of reasoning is quite disappointing. As far as I can tell, it simply assumes that we need ethical virtue in order to recognize the end. Saying that only virtuous people can see the end correctly might be true, but it is rhetorically powerless because it seems to beg the question. Once we have made the end ethical, it is obvious that good people would see it better. The question is, why should the others care?

ANOTHER APPROACH: INSTRUMENTAL REASON

In a life according to reason, reason rules and is never merely instrumental. It shapes desire and directs activity with an eye to the highest end. The bad person misidentifies the *telos* because he does not understand that rational activity is the highest end and thus does not aim at fully developing his nature. He mistakenly assumes that rational activity is merely a means of getting other things, such as money and honor. His failure to know the highest end shows that he is not fully rational. He lacks the understanding of the *phronimos* concerning the proper ordering of ends. The man who reduces reason to the level of a mere instrument thereby exhibits his incomplete rationality. And because he is not fully rational, he will not perform the human function well and he will not attain normative *eudaimonia*. His lack of *phronêsis* impairs his performance of the human function.

Can we show him that he is wrong in taking reason to be instrumental? Irwin suggests that we can, arguing that Aristotle's argument concerning the nature of a rational agent can be extended to show that a rational agent must take rational activity to be an end in itself. Irwin shares my view that any rational agent must embrace at least an instrumental need for at least some of the virtues, but he argues that a consideration of rational nature can take us much further, establishing that it is in our own interest to develop the ethical virtues:

> To develop a virtue is to express our essence as rational and responsible agents, and to that extent the cultivation of virtues must be part of a rational agent's good. . . .
>
> If I rationally choose to form a state of character that reduces the role of my rational agency in my action, I am choosing not to realize my nature as a rational agent any further. But if I choose this in my

own interest, I am being inconsistent; for if I understand my own interest, I must understand my own essence; and if this consists in rational agency, I am inconsistent if I choose in my own interest not to realize my own essence. (1989, 374)

The relevant portion of Irwin's argument seems to take the following form: To act in my own interest is to realize my own essence. Therefore, if rational activity and the cultivation of virtue are to realize my own essence (which they are), then to neglect them or give it merely instrumental value is to neglect my own interest, which would be self-contradictory.

In my view, the basic problem in the argument lies in the very first step: As I have argued throughout, there seems to be no rationally compelling reason for the opponent to accept the project of realizing his own essence; he has no reason to agree that this project is what is in his own interest. Irwin responds to similar complaints by arguing that a consideration of the very nature of a rational agent shows that he must care about developing his capacities. In order to be persuaded by Aristotle's argument, then, I do not need a proper upbringing which has taught me to love the fine. I merely need to think of myself as essentially a rational agent. The relevant portion of his reconstruction of Aristotle's argument (1989, 366–67) has four steps that I paraphrase as follows:

1. To be a rational agent involves having a conception of what is best to do which includes a consideration of one's future, not just one's current desires and needs.
2. This means that I must think about my desires and try to balance them. A rational agent will try to fulfill "more rather than fewer [desires], . . . other things being equal."
3. This also means that I must think about my capacities, determining which ones I should actualize. As with desires, the rational agent must attempt to fulfill "more rather than fewer" of them, "other things being equal." A failure to do that is to fail to take the whole self into account.
4. If I fail to try to develop my capacities, then, I am involved in self-contradiction, failing to "act on the consequences of principles [I] already accept."

I agree with Irwin's first two steps, but I disagree with the final two. It is obvious that I will care about fulfilling my desires. Indeed, it is trivially true because fulfilling my desires is getting what I want—which of course is exactly what I want. However, there does not seem to be a parallel argument for developing my capacities. Why exactly must I be interested in developing my capacities? We can easily develop an argument for why we should take an instrumental interest in our capacities, just as we were able to show why I must take an instrumental interest in some of the virtues. In order to fulfill my desires, I will need to actualize some of my capacities (learning French so that I can read Sartre in the original perhaps). However, Irwin argues that I also should care about developing my capacities for the sake of developing them or for the sake of making myself into a better and more well-rounded person. I agree, but I do not believe that those who disagree are involved in self-contradiction. For Irwin's argument to work, it seems to me, we have to assume that people have an additional desire, a desire for developing capacities or for being all they can be. This seems quite similar to saying that they need to care about normative rather than merely conative *eudaimonia*. The problem is identical: we are not rationally compelled to care about this. If we do care, neglecting development of our capacities would indeed involve us in self-contradiction. But if we do not, there seems to be no contradiction. And the problem with the bad man is exactly that he does not care. Finally, even if he does care about developing his capacities, getting him interested in the virtue of character is another and very large step. The bad theoretician illustrates this point. He certainly recognizes the intrinsic value of reason and passionately wants to develop his intellectual capacities, but he has little or no interest in the virtues of character.

So where do we stand, at the end of this discussion? I have suggested that most of Aristotle's argument in Book 1 is powerful and persuasive. He makes a strong case for the thesis that an action is truly in accordance with reason only if it aims at the highest end (or if it aims at a lower end as a means to that end) and for saying that the highest end is *eudaimonia*. The trouble begins when we look to him to prove that *eudaimonia* is not just conative but normative and that it includes the virtues. The function argument provides a plausible account of normative *eudaimonia*. However, it has two important limitations: First, it does not show that *eudaimonia* construed in this way is indeed the end I should pursue. The skeptic and the bad person can and should easily retort to Aristotle's argument by pointing out that Aristotle assumes that they have accepted normative *eudaimonia* as their highest end, which they have not. Aristotle is saying that only a person with ethical virtue will recognize the highest end; only he will see that normative *eudaimonia* is what we ought to pursue. What remains to be shown, however, and what Aristotle does not show, is that we have compelling reasons to make the highest end our end. Similarly, Irwin does not show why we should aim at developing our capacities. Unless we accept normative *eudaimonia* as our end, knowing that we are not discerning *eudaimonia* in the way the virtuous person does will not distress us but will seem to be evidence of our unclouded vision. Consequently, it seems to me, the skeptic should respond by saying something like the following: "You are begging the question by assuming that the ethical virtues enable us to see better. I see no reason to accept your assumption. Perhaps they distort our vision; perhaps they make us see worse and not better. I agree that they sometimes are useful, and to that limited extent, I will pursue them. I will also agree with you that if you are virtuous, you will see normative *eudaimonia* or self-development as the highest end. But I have no reason to accept that this is the correct way of viewing the highest end." In other words, Aristotle has not provided sufficient reason for people to abandon their original *telos* (conative *eudaimonia*).

Second, Aristotle makes a strong case for an instrumental defense of the virtues, but he does not show why they must be part of the end. As McDowell notes, the *ergon* argument does not establish that the virtuous man is better than the one focusing on his own best interest (1980, 366), somebody who believes that "genuine human excellence is the intelligence and strength needed to further one's own selfish ends" (1980, 374 n.17). It also does not refute the bad theoretician's view that theoretical wisdom is the only important and intrinsically valuable kind of human excellence.[19] Aristotle is basing his argument on a conceptual link between *aretê* and *ergon*, but the link does not hold between ethical virtue and *ergon*. Put differently, his argument does not settle disputes between competing conceptions of excellence.

If our goal is to find an argument in the *Ethics* that would persuade any rational person of the intrinsic value of rational activity and of the ethical virtues, we have failed. Indeed, Aristotle's argument there fails to persuade some of the most rational people of all, people of eminent intelligent excellence. In the final chapter, I will show that other arguments will fail to persuade bad men as well, that Aristotle recognized this limitation of arguments, and that persuading bad men was never his goal. I will suggest that his attitude was reasonable and that we would do well to adopt it.

chapter five

ANSWERING THOSE WHO DO NOT LOVE THE FINE

We have considered Aristotle's Book I argument, and I have argued that it cannot prove to the skeptic and the bad man that they must adopt that human end as their own end because it fails to prove to them that they are wrong in neglecting normative *eudaimonia* or in viewing virtue as merely instrumental. In this chapter, I will argue that other arguments will fail in similar ways and that Aristotle was well aware of this. I will first consider the possibility of arguing to ethics from human nature and from *eudaimonia*. I will suggest that both involve serious difficulties: If we start with human nature or conative *eudaimonia*, we will have premises that the bad man could accept, but it seems impossible to derive an ethics from them; ethics is supposed to correct human nature and desires and thus cannot be derived from it. If we start from normative *eudaimonia*, on the other hand, we should be able to derive an ethics. However, we can do that only because by starting from normative *eudaimonia*, we have already included considerations which the bad man has no compelling reason to accept. Thus, in his view, our argument will seem viciously circular. In addition, I will argue, suggesting that Aristotle argued from *eudaimonia* (conative or normative) to the virtues seems to invert the relationship he saw between the two.

I will also consider the status of the why which I have previously argued that the good man must possess. It is tempting to assume that this why could serve as the argument we are seeking. I will argue that this is not so because it will presuppose the that. Thus, the why will have limitations similar to the arguments already discussed; it will proceed from the that and thus will have no effect on those lacking the that. Having outlined the inadequacy of all these arguments, I will argue that Aristotle was well aware of the difficulties involved in persuading the bad man. I will base this thesis upon a consideration of how and why Aristotle limits his audience and of his view of decision making.[1] The problem is that any argument for ethics will need to appeal to a combination of reason and desire, and a person who does not have appropriate desires will not be persuaded. Thus, the failure of the various arguments is unavoidable. Finally, I will consider how seriously we should take this failure. What are its implications? Can we still be held responsible for our character, and can reflection lead to moral improvement, or is the basis of ethics too irrational for this to be possible? I will deny that our failure means that our commitment to ethics is fundamentally irrational, following Williams and McDowell in arguing that we should reexamine our desire for proof. However, I will argue against Williams that reflection still can and must play a crucial part in moral improvement and that most of us can and should be held responsible for our character.

STARTING FROM FIRST OR SECOND HUMAN NATURE

It is tempting to believe that Aristotle argued for ethics from his understanding of human nature. If we understand what we are, we will understand why we should be ethical. What is natural for us determines what we should do. But how might this argument work? One of the obvious problems with trying to use human nature as a grounding for ethics is that human nature does not seem very *good*. Doing what is natural is not always right. Indeed, many actions that are natural for human beings—in the sense of stemming from powerful human impulses—are morally questionable or simply wrong (rape, slavery, and infidelity). Williams puts the point as follows:

> If it is a mark of a man to employ intelligence and tools in modifying his environment, it is equally a mark of him to employ intelligence in getting his own way and tools in destroying others. If it is a mark of a man to have a conceptualized and fully conscious awareness of himself as one among others, aware that others have feelings like himself, this is a precondition not only of benevolence but (as Nietzsche pointed out) of cruelty as well. (1976, 59–60)

Aristotle himself recognizes that some natural tendencies are problematic: "Since, for example, we have more of a natural tendency to pleasure, we drift more easily toward intemperance than toward orderliness. Hence we say that an extreme is more contrary [to the mean] if we naturally develop more in that direction" (1109a16). We naturally want pleasure, but that is a want that needs to be tempered: "We must beware above all of pleasure and its sources; for we are already biased in its favor" (1109b8–9). That is, we have certain natural inclinations that we do not want to encourage, much less make into standards for behavior. Many of our natural inclinations may be good, but some of the actions that are in our nature should be avoided, and some aspects of our natural character must be reshaped and moderated.

But if many parts of human nature are bad and need to be corrected, how can our nature determine what we should do? To answer, we must first follow Irwin and others in noticing that Aristotle uses two senses of "nature" and "natural."[2] I will refer to them as first and second nature. What is natural in the first sense is what we are born with, what is usually present in human beings apart from human intervention. In contrast, the second sense refers to fully developed human nature, nature which has reached its *telos* and in which the human form is fully actualized. In other words, it refers to human nature in somebody who is performing the human function excellently.

Now, as I argued above, first nature is unsuitable as a grounding for ethics because what is natural in the first sense is not always right. If we were trying to ground ethics in human nature, we would not start with the fact that we are the only animal that makes war on its own or that we often are jealous, that we torture other human beings or that we often are selfish. Rather, we might note that we are rational, that we are social, and that we can form close friendships. That is, we would select good facts about nature. In order to be able to do that, we need a distinction between good and bad already in place. Therefore, we cannot also use first nature to generate that distinction. Indeed, trying to do so seems to misunderstand the relation between ethics and human nature. The point of ethics is to control and modify first nature.[3] But then, ethics cannot be derived from first nature. Rather, ethics guides us as we transform our first nature into second nature, developing the tendencies of first nature that belong in second nature and getting rid of the ones that do not.

Perhaps our argument could begin instead with second nature and argue for an ethics from that. Second nature is the *telos* towards which we develop; it is what is actualized in us when and if we become fully developed. In other words, it is *eudaimonia*. Hence, could we not argue to ethics from *eudaimonia*, suggesting that *eudaimonia* provides the motivation for ethical action, giving us an argument for why we should bother being ethical? We should be ethical because being ethical is a necessary part of happiness. Contemporary virtue ethics seems to proceed in this way and to have traced this approach back to Aristotle. In the past, this has been a common reading of Aristotle.[4] On this reading, Aristotle views *eudaimonia* as the prior notion, and then derives virtues from it. Virtues are the qualities that promote our happiness.

In my view, any attempt to defend ethics based on *eudaimonia* is deeply problematic. First, neither conative nor normative *eudaimonia* is suited for this task. It is obvious, I think, that we cannot ground ethics in conative happiness; there is no reason to think that ethics will be a necessary part of such happiness, or that it always or even usually will be a means to it. I could certainly derive a code of behavior from what I want and desire. The problem is that this code is unlikely to be an ethics in any recognizable sense, and since wants and desires often differ from person to person, different people would not end up with the same code. On the other hand, we can, of course, argue from the normative definition of *eudaimonia*—virtuous activity—to the conclusion that *eudaimonia* requires virtue. But a person who needs to be persuaded that he should aim for the fine and that he should take an interest in virtue will not embrace normative happiness as his end. Rather, he will quite reasonably respond that the argument begs the question. In other words, the attempt to ground ethics in normative *eudaimonia* seems unavoidably circular. Unlike conative *eudaimonia*, normative *eudaimonia* is not an ideal that we naturally embrace. In addition, we have also seen that even if we accept normative *eudaimonia* as the highest end, we can still neglect ethics for the sake of *theôria*. For us to see and agree with Aristotle that happiness requires ethical virtue, we must already be at least sort of virtuous; we must already love the fine. Otherwise, we will not accept his definition of *eudaimonia*.

The attempted grounding of ethics in *eudaimonia* is also troubling for a second reason. As Kant famously objected, it seems to relegate virtue to an instrumental position as a mere means to happiness. Kant aside, such a reading misunderstands Aristotle's view of the relation between *eudaimonia* and virtue. Rather than using virtue as a means to happiness, Aristotle seems to embrace Kant's criticism, insisting that the good man acts for the sake of virtue no less than for the sake of happiness:

> Honor, pleasure, understanding, and every virtue we certainly choose
> because of themselves, since we would choose each of them even if it

had no further result; but we also choose them for the sake of happiness. (1097b3–4)

The noble [*kalon*], then, is that which, being desirable in itself, is at the same time worthy of praise. (*Rhetoric* 1366a)

As I argued in chapter 1, the virtuous man is virtuous precisely because he has adopted the fine as his highest end and then modified his understanding of his other ends (the pleasant and the useful) accordingly. He does not pursue the fine as a means to happiness; he pursues the fine for its own sake. If he viewed fine action as a means and not as an intrinsic end, he would not even be continent but would belong among the many who perform fine action out of fear or in order to be honored.

Aristotle takes the virtues to be *ta pros ta tele*, "towards" the end of happiness, but it has often and rightly been pointed out that he does not regard them as simple means. If virtues are means to happiness, they are means to an end that in part consists of virtuous activity because Aristotle defines *eudaimonia* as "activity of the soul in accord with virtue" (1098a17). In other words, as numerous scholars have noted, Aristotle views virtues as constituent means to happiness.[5] Thus, when MacIntyre writes that "the virtues are precisely those qualities the possession of which will enable an individual to achieve *eudaimonia*" (1984, 148), what he says is true but it is also misleading because it makes it seem as though *eudaimonia* is the prior and more basic notion, and it suggests that the virtues are defined in terms of happiness. As MacIntyre recognizes that is not so—it is the other way around. In Annas's words, "happiness is the vague notion that has to bend to that of virtue" (1993, 331). We must turn to virtue to understand happiness, not vice versa. Aristotle writes: "Since happiness is a certain sort of activity of the soul in accord with complete virtue, we must examine virtue; for that will perhaps also be a way to study happiness better" (1102a5–7). Happiness is impossible without virtue, because virtue is part of happiness, and virtue requires engaging in fine actions for the sake of the fine, not just for the sake of happiness. It is important to note that the impossibility is not just an impossibility such that given the state of the world it happens to be so. Rather, Aristotle believes that it is impossible on a conceptual level because being virtuous is part of what it means to be *eudaimôn*.[6] To construe him as arguing from normative *eudaimonia* to ethics thus distorts the relationship between the two because it suggests that *eudaimonia* and not virtue is the fundamental notion.

The same message regarding the relation between virtue and happiness also emerges from a curious passage in 1.9 where Aristotle asks whether happiness is a divine gift or if it is acquired by virtue and answers that it is acquired by virtue. Why? He replies: "Since it is better to be happy in this way than because of fortune, it is reasonable for this to be the way [we become] happy. For whatever is natural is naturally in the finest state possible" (1099b22–23). In this passage, Aristotle seems to argue from how it would be best for things to be to what is natural, from what the link between virtue and happiness should be to what it is. That is, Aristotle is not inferring ought from is. If anything, he is moving in the opposite direction, getting is from ought. It is better that we become happy through virtue rather than through fortune, so it must be so. Why is it better to become happy through virtue than through fortune? Aristotle says that it is better because "it would be seriously inappropriate to entrust what is greatest and finest to fortune" (1099b24). The line of thinking here is reminiscent of his arguments for the principle of non-contradiction in the *Metaphysics* and the beginning of the *Ethics* where Aristotle says that unless things were in a certain way, our desire would be empty and vain. The common thread is the conviction that the world has to be a good place that makes sense. A link between happiness and virtue makes the world fairer than it would be if the gods randomly bestowed happiness on some and not on others. Instead of being an undeserved divine gift, Aristotle insists, happiness must be something that is within our power (although not completely) and it must be up to us if we are going to get there or not. "Anyone who is not deformed [in his capacity] for virtue will be able to achieve happiness through some sort of learning and attention" (1099b18–20). We cannot be happy without being virtuous.

It appears, then, that neither first nor second nature can provide a suitable grounding for ethics. First nature fails because it is too ambiguous. While it contains tendencies that ethics will foster (altruism, kindness, and so on), it also contains tendencies that ethics is designed to combat (selfishness, greed). Second nature fails because it is already ethical; using it to argue for ethics introduces circularity. Finally, the idea of arguing to ethics from *eudaimonia* gets Aristotle backwards. Aristotle does not think that we should accept his idea of virtue because it follows from his idea of *eudaimonia*. Rather, we should accept his idea of *eudaimonia* because it encapsulates virtue as well as common sense notions of what it is to live well.

THE LIMITATIONS OF THE WHY

Now, in previous chapters, I have argued that the good man must know the why. That is, he must know not only what he should do but also why that is the correct thing to do. One might think that this why could serve as an argument for the that, providing a justification of our habituated ethical beliefs. However, I will argue, it provides only internal justification, which is available only to those who already possess certain promises. The difficulty here is connected to the issue of starting points. Aristotle argues that reasoning must either begin from or move toward starting points or principles (*archai*) and he states that in ethical discussions, we "ought to begin from things known to *us*" (1095a32–b4). The source of starting points varies depending on the subject, but in the case of human actions and ethical reasoning, we get them through habituation. Later in the *Ethics*, Aristotle specifies by saying that the starting point in human action is the end we act for (1151a15). This suggests that we will have a hierarchy of starting points available to us, the highest of which should be normative *eudaimonia*, the human end.[7] (Because of the close relationship between *eudaimonia* and the fine, we could equally well argue that the *archê* in question should be the fine.)

I say "should" because other starting points are possible. A person who is incorrectly habituated will not have the correct highest principle. As I have argued, the problem with the bad person is exactly that he does not view normative *eudaimonia* as his end. Rather, his highest *archê* will be conative *eudaimonia*. In addition, because the principle is not static, our lifestyle can affect it. Virtue and vice preserve and corrupt the principle so that even a well-habituated person might lose the principle and become unable to discern the end if he repeatedly acts badly. Put differently, he will no longer recognize normative *eudaimonia* as his highest principle and will become just like the poorly habituated person. All this is expressed in the following crucial passage:

For virtue preserves the principle, whereas vice corrupts it; and in actions the end we act for is the principle, as the assumptions are the principles in mathematics. Reason does not teach the principles either in mathematics or in actions; [with actions] it is virtue, either natural or habituated, that teaches correct belief about the principle. (1151a15–19)

Reason's dependence upon starting points that we acquire through proper habituation has significant consequences. It means that arguments cannot persuade those who have not been habituated properly, no matter how rational they are, because all our arguments have to rely upon these starting points.

We can look back at our previous arguments and see how this difficulty emerges again and again. The argument from second nature discussed earlier in this chapter fails because its starting point—normative *eudaimonia*—is not shared by the bad man nor for the sake of his argument by the skeptic. Aristotle's Book 1 argument works if we believe that normative *eudaimonia* is our end, but it does not and cannot show that each individual is rationally compelled to believe that. In chapter 4, I argued that Aristotle does not provide a sufficient argument for why we should accept his notion of *eudaimonia* as our highest end. We can see now that Aristotle would dismiss this as a naïve complaint; *eudaimonia* is a starting point and, as such, it is not a conclusion of an argument, but a premise. In the *Eudemian Ethics*, he remarks: "Nobody *proves* that health is a good (unless he is a sophist and not a physician—it is sophists that juggle with irrelevant arguments), any more than he proves any other first principle" (*EE* 1218b22–24).

More generally, our various arguments for why we should be ethical start from a that that is and must be acquired through habituation. They are arguments *from* principles. Arguing in this way follows the procedure Aristotle recommends, beginning with what is known to us (1095a32–34). But as Aristotle makes clear, this procedure has a high cost: our argument will not persuade all. He continues: "[The need to start from what is known to us] is why we need to have been brought up in fine habits if we are to be adequate students of fine and just things, and of political questions generally. For we begin from the [belief] that [something is true]; if this is apparent enough to us, we can begin without also [knowing] why [it is true]. Someone who is well brought up either has the beginnings [*archas*], or can easily acquire them" (1095b5–9). A person who has been properly brought up will know what *eudaimonia* truly is, and he will love the fine. From that starting point, he can come to understand why normative *eudaimonia* should be his goal. But if he lacks this starting point, he cannot: "For inferences about actions have a principle, 'Since the end and the best good is this sort of thing' (whatever it actually is—let it be any old thing for the sake of argument). And this [best good] is apparent only to the good person; for vice perverts us and produces false views about the principles of action" (1144a30–36).

As McDowell notes, we might conceive of a why as either providing validation from the outside or from the inside (1995a, 213). The former kind of why gives an external foundation; the latter operates as a coherentist confirmation, enabling the agent to see how his "hitherto separate perceptions of what situations call for hang together, so that acting on them can be seen as putting into practice a coherent scheme for a life" (1995a, 213). When Aristotle indicates that the good person knows why he should be ethical or why he should do *x* rather than *y*, then, he does not mean that the good person can prove this to the skeptic. He cannot give an external foundation. Rather, Aristotle's view seems to be that the why provides validation from the inside for actions that previously may have seemed to be imposed from without by parents or societal expectation. To know the that is to know what should be done in the particular case; to know the why is to know how the particular action fits into one's life as a whole and how it contributes to *eudaimonia* and to the *kalon*. More generally, it is to understand why virtues and love of the fine are appropriate and how they are related to the human *telos*.

McDowell suggests that we might conceive of acquiring the why in terms of Neurath's sailor (1995a, 213), a metaphor which I find quite helpful. Just as the Neurathian sailor cannot bring the boat ashore for repair but must keep it afloat while fixing it, using only the materials already on the boat, so we have "no material to exploit in defending our ethics except the initially unreflective perceptions of the *that* from which reflection starts" (1995a, 213). We cannot get outside the knowledge of a good person to some objective, value-neutral shore.

PROPER AUDIENCE, BAD MEN, AND SKEPTICS

A consideration of how and why Aristotle limits his audience provides additional reasons for denying that Aristotle was trying to provide an argument for ethics that could persuade the bad man of the error of his ways. Indeed, it suggests that Aristotle was well aware of the difficulties involved. If Aristotle had thought that he had an extra-ethical grounding for ethics, an answer to the bad man, his intended audience would have included all rational human beings.[8] All people who could hear and understand his words should have been included. However, Aristotle makes clear that he is not talking to everybody but rather to a more narrow segment of humanity, namely to those who have been properly educated. (I'll make his selection criteria more precise in a moment.) He excludes all others, arguing that they do not benefit from hearing ethical discourses.

Who is excluded and on what grounds? Critics sometimes suggest that Aristotle's audience is restricted to Athenian gentleman. I do not think that is so. Rather, his audiences are those who love the fine, those who see ethics as a motive for action. They are sort of good, at least, have their desires under some control, and are therefore open to being improved through listening to and acting upon a *logos*. The goal of his writing and lecturing is to modify the behavior of the listeners—but listeners who are already within the ethical and who need their behavior and ideas polished rather than radically remade (see 1095a10). They do not have to share exactly the same view of the *telos* (they may disagree about the proper list of virtues for instance), but they must believe that the fine is part of that end. Between people who share that starting point, dialogue and argument are possible and potentially fruitful.

Aristotle discusses the appropriate audience for ethical discussions in two parts of the *Ethics*: 1.3–4 and 10.9. In 1.3, he writes that his listeners should be people who "accord with reason in forming their desires" (1095a10), and he excludes young people because they follow their feelings rather than reason. In 1.4, he adds that his listeners "need to have been brought up in fine habits" (1095b5–6). In 10.9, which constitutes the transition to the *Politics*, Aristotle again suggests that we must have gone through certain preparation in order to be suitable listeners:

> Arguments and teaching surely do not prevail on everyone, but the soul of the student needs to have been prepared by habits for enjoying and hating finely, like ground that is to nourish seed. For someone who lives in accord with his feelings would not even listen to an argument turning him away, or comprehend it [if he did listen]; and in that state how could he be persuaded to change? And in general feelings seem to yield to force, not to argument. Hence we must already in some way have a character suitable for virtue, fond of what is fine and objecting to what is shameful. (1179b24–30)

Taken together, these texts sketch the suitable listeners, giving them the following characteristics:

1. brought up in fine habits
2. accord with reason in forming their desires
3. led by reason rather than feelings

4. have characters suitable for virtue: fond of what is fine and objecting to what is shameful
5. experienced

I will set the issue of experience to one side and focus upon the rest of the characteristics that, I believe, really express one complex condition. A person who is brought up in fine habits (1) has learned to form her desires in accordance with reason (2). Her soul is ruled by *logos* so she tends to follow reason rather than feelings when she acts (3). Consequently, she has a character suitable for virtue (4).

What is Aristotle's line of thought here? Part of his reasoning seems psychological. Consider young people. Aristotle excludes them from the appropriate audience because they are guided by their feelings rather than by reason (1095a3–5). Discourse might indeed change their thinking about how they should live. However, it will not change their behavior because they have not yet learned to be guided by reason.[9] They have to learn that first. If we are going to alter behavior through persuasion, we need to persuade whatever is in charge, so if desires and cravings are in charge, pleading with reason does no good. Incontinent people need to be retrained; arguing with them is pointless.

But of course, bad people are not necessarily incontinent. Some of them are perfectly capable of acting in accordance with reason. Changing their views, then, ought to lead to a change in behavior. Aristotle excludes them, too, because he believes that his hearers must already be fond of what is fine: "We must already in some way have a character suitable for virtue, fond of what is fine and disliking what is shameful" (1179b29–30). To be an appropriate audience, then, we must love the fine and hate the shameful, and we must aim at the fine. Those who do not are not a suitable audience for Aristotle's discussion. They first must acquire a new set of motives, a desire to act for the sake of the fine as well as a love of the fine, and this is done through habituation, not teaching.

If the fine has not become part of their motivational make-up, trying to persuade them of the value of ethics is pointless. Those who have not come to see things other than their own pleasure and gain as motives, for example, cannot be swayed by Aristotle's arguments because they will not accept its basic premise (the human end). Thus, he excludes them from his audience. The bad man's inability to recognize the end is not due to stupidity or irrationality. Still, Aristotle argues that the bad man's reasoning is defective. He notes that it may at first seem that the bad person reasons correctly: "The

incontinent or base person will use rational calculation to reach what he pro-
poses to see, and so will have deliberated correctly [if that is all it takes] but
will have got himself a great evil" (1142b20). In other words, he is quite capable of using reason and deliberating effectively to reach his ends and to
fulfill his desires. However, Aristotle thinks that correct deliberation in fact
requires more than successful means/ends reasoning. Correct deliberation
must aim at a good. More precisely, it must be informed by a desire to reach
the human *telos*. It must reach a good, and it must hit upon the right thing
to do: "Unqualifiedly good deliberation is the sort that correctly promotes the
unqualified end [i.e., the highest good], while the [limited] sort is the sort
that correctly promoted some [limited] end" (1142b30–32). This means that
Aristotle can deny that the bad person deliberates correctly, but he can do so
only by allowing correct deliberation to become imbued with an ethical
sense. Good deliberation cannot lead to an unethical decision because it
requires more than correct reasoning; it must also be informed by good
desires. Consequently, bad men do not reason well because they lack the
proper motivation. The difference between good and bad people is not that
the former have understood an argument that the latter have not, or that the
latter are incontinent. Rather, the problem with bad people is that they are
aiming for the wrong thing, and they are aiming for the wrong thing because
they want the wrong thing, and they want the wrong thing because their
desires are poorly trained.

We cannot argue people into acquiring a wholly new set of motives
because arguments do not make people care about the fine. Aristotle em-
phasizes this point in 10.9:

> Arguments seem to have enough influence to stimulate and encourage
> the civilized ones among the young people, and perhaps to make virtue
> take possession of a well-born character that truly loves what is fine,
> but they seem unable to turn the many toward being fine and good.
> (1179b8–10)

If we already love the fine, we are likely to benefit from ethical conversations
(I'll return to this point later). If we do not, arguments have no effect. Trying
to argue Thrasymachus into ethics is a waste of time. In order to prove to
him that he should acquire ethical motives, we would have to convince him
that it is in his interest to do so. That is, we would have to show him that it
serves motives that he already has. For example, we might show him that
ethical motives are pleasant or profitable, or that they will make him

respected and admired. However, such an approach simply would not work because fine actions are often not in our self-interest in this sense. On the contrary, fine motives are likely to force us to risk our lives, to share goods, and to rule the city when we would rather not.[10]

We reach the same conclusion if we start from Aristotle's view that good decisions require both true reason and correct desire (1139a22). If Aristotle is right in saying that good decisions require both true reason and correct desire, we cannot give compelling arguments to the skeptic and the bad man for why we should be good. In trying to provide such arguments, we ignore one of the two parts of decision making; we eliminate correct desire and retain true reason, saying that reason by itself should be capable of making ethical decisions. But reason by itself has no goals or purposes, so it cannot decide or make us act without help.[11] It needs a goal: What is the point, what are we after? Aristotle argues that there is a human *telos* that we should pursue, but the bad person will not recognize it as his own *telos*. Indeed, his failure to do so is exactly what is wrong with him. Due to his vicious nature, he lacks the needed principle (*archê*). Thus, while (some) bad people would be able to figure out how to reach the human *telos* if the task were presented to them as a hypothetical problem, they do not recognize it as their own end and consequently will not strive to reach it. We cannot prove to them that they are wrong because our arguments must use that fundamental principle as a starting point, and they either never had that principle or have lost it due to their vicious actions. Because they do not love the fine, they do not aim at normative *eudaimonia*.

Still, bad men can become good and arguments may play a role in their conversion. For example, arguments (ours or ones that he himself discovers) may persuade a bad man of the instrumental value of virtue, for instance, by persuading him that an unethical life often has undesirable consequences (jail, premature death, etc.) which an ethical life avoids. Once he starts practicing virtue for instrumental reasons, he might come to view virtue as worthwhile in its own right.[12]

IMPROVEMENT THROUGH REFLECTION

The *Ethics* is not intended to convert the bad man because Aristotle recognizes that no book and no argument can do that. But it still has a significant role to play because to say that we cannot convince the bad man is very different from saying that we cannot present arguments at all. While Aristotle dismisses the project of convincing the bad man, he is still trying to show the rest of us what the bad man is missing. We cannot answer the bad man, but we can still talk about him and perhaps even understand him better than he understands himself, although of course, he will not agree that we do. In addition, we do not have to give up on both interlocutors from the *Republic*. Unlike discussions with the bad man, discussions with the skeptic can be fruitful. The proper response to Glaucon's skeptical demand for a justification for ethics that does not use his love of the fine as a starting point is to say that his demand is unreasonable. Then, one might go to argue for a particular way of life, explaining what living well consists in for human beings and discussing some of the obstacles we encounter along the way and show how the parts of goodness fit together once we have become good. It seems to me that this is exactly what Aristotle's ethics does. The *Ethics* provides a why to those who already love the fine by showing how virtue and virtuous action fit into the good life.[13] While the *Ethics* cannot make a bad person good, it can help a good person become better through helping her to increase her understanding of herself, her actions, and the *telos* of her life and encouraging her to make herself better.[14] Thus, its intended audience is ordinary people who are sometimes continent and often incontinent. It attempts to reinforce their belief that they should be ethical by providing reasons for why that is so and by showing the lack in bad men. It also aims to inspire the members of the audience to improve themselves: "Our present discussion does not aim, as others do, at study; for the purpose of our examination is not to know what virtue is, but to become good, since otherwise the inquiry would be of no benefit to us" (1103b28–29). We are called upon to reflect upon our lives, see where we are weak, and then improve. A rational recognition of our deficiencies will lead us to change.

But is this a realistic task? To what extent is such recognition and improvement really possible, given the significant role of desire and habituation in ethical development? Can we come to recognize our flaws and then work to change based on that recognition? The first difficulty is that since our character formation begins in early childhood, some habits will be firmly in place before reason is able to ask whether they are good or bad. By the time I am mature enough to ask, my character already has a predominantly good—or bad—shape. I have learned to desire good or bad things; I have acquired simple or extravagant tastes. I have acquired the right or the wrong beginnings. I have learned to love the fine—or I have not. But if all this is so, radical change based upon self-examination seems impossible. Williams writes:

Aristotle should not have believed that in the most basic respects, at least, people were responsible for their characters. He gives an account of moral development in terms of habituation and internalization that leaves little room for practical reason to alter radically the objectives that a grown-up person has acquired. (1985, 38)

Williams is right in pointing out that it is unreasonable for Aristotle to hold that people who were fundamentally miseducated are responsible for who they became. Aristotle argues that one's character determines how the end appears but he refuses to use this to excuse people: "If each person is in some way responsible for his own state [of character], he is also himself in some way responsible for how [the end] appears" (1114b3–5). He acknowledges that the bad person may be incapable of becoming other than what he is. The intemperate person, for example, is incurable (1150b30–35). To Aristotle, this does not change the fact that he is culpable for his actions and for his character. He is responsible for what he is not now free to change, because at one point he was free to become or not become what he now is and because what is compelling him is his own character.

But as Williams rightly argues, it is not clear why we should think that such a person was free to become who he is. On the contrary, it seems clear that he was not. Aristotle is arguing that we do and should hold people responsible for the result of an educational training process that began when they were too young to know what was happening. People are responsible for not seeing the end even if bad training in early childhood made them blind. Thus, Williams is right in noting that Aristotle's account of ethical responsibility is too severe and too ready to condemn people for what was done to them. It simply does not seem to be true that such blinded people were at one point capable of becoming other than they became. Of course, they could have turned out differently (by having other parents, living in another city, and so on), but I do not see how they could be expected to know enough as young children to make themselves turn out differently. Rather, who they became seems to be due to external forces acting upon them. The appropriate response would seem to be to ask whether sight can be restored, not to blame them for not seeing.

However, while it is unreasonable to fault those for whom the entire framework is missing or to assume that they would see the errors of their ways if they just looked harder, most of us are luckily not in that position. It seems to me that the more interesting question is what responsibility we can assign to those of us who have the basic principles and to what extent reflection can inspire improvement in us. Williams raises difficulties here too, suggesting that an individual's reflection upon her life will not make her better, because by the time she is mature enough to engage in such reflection, her character is already in place. He introduces the problem by suggesting that Aristotle's presentation of his inquiry is problematic:

> He makes it seem as though you can review the whole of your life and consider whether it was aimed in the most worthwhile direction, but, on his own account, this cannot be a sensible picture. . . . One becomes virtuous or fails to do so only through habituation. One should not study moral philosophy until middle age. . . . But by then it will be a long time since one became, in relation to this deliberation, preemptively good or irrecoverably bad. (1985, 39)

Williams concludes:

> Aristotle cannot reasonably believe that his reflections on the virtuous life and its role in helping to constitute well-being could play a formative part in some general deliberation that a given person might conduct . . . . [T]he answer to Socrates' question [of how we should live] cannot be used by those who (from the perspective of the rest) most need it. (Ibid. 39–40)

If the task of the *Ethics* is to improve people by making them reflect, then, it is bound to fail. It becomes unclear why Aristotle thinks that knowledge of the good would have an important, practical function.[15] Reflection cannot change bad people and good people do not need changing.

It seems to me that Williams misstates the issue in two ways. First, he makes it seem as though good and bad are jointly exhaustive alternatives. They are not. Rather, goodness and badness are on a continuum from ethical perfection at the top to utter perversity at the bottom. It is true that a person who is at either extreme will not improve by reflection: The person who is perfectly good cannot improve since he is already perfect, and the person who is perfectly bad cannot improve himself since he is beyond hope.[16] However, most of us are in between the two extremes, good at some things and not so good at others, and reflection will enable us to inch upward on that continuum.[17]

Second, Williams suggests that we first are habituated and then reflect upon the result. As already noted, I do not think that Aristotle takes the two to be quite so separate. Rather, reflection should begin before habituation is completed, as our education becomes more and more intellectual, reflective, and philosophical, and habituation does not end when we turn eighteen or twenty-five—or even fifty. This is implied by one of Aristotle's comments in his discussion of the many: "It is not enough if they get the correct upbringing and attention when they are young; rather, they must continue the same practices and be habituated to them when they become men" (1180a1–3). Theoretically, habituation ends when we become perfect (when we have actually reached the *telos*), but since human beings will never become perfect, training will never end. Given the need for continuous improvement and lifelong habituation, the Aristotelian belief that I am responsible for my character and also able and obliged to improve it is useful and beneficial. The person who can begin to understand her own character and its deficiencies can and should seek to become better. If I have not learned courage, for instance, I might still as an adult come to recognize this as a deficiency in me and set about to change. Sometimes, external circumstances might lead to recognition of deficiency. In *The Screwtape Letters*, C. S. Lewis plays ghost-writer for the devil Screwtape, and gives a pertinent example: "We have made men proud of most vices, but not of cowardice. Whenever we have almost succeeded in doing so, the Enemy [God] permits a war or an earthquake or some other calamity, and at once courage becomes so obviously lovely and important even in human eyes that all our work is undone, and there is still at least one vice of which they feel genuine shame" (1960, 147–48). In other words, a situation that arises might make the value of courage apparent, thereby forcing some people to examine themselves, find themselves deficient, and ask what they can do to make themselves more courageous. But the same circumstance might not have that effect on another person, and in some people's lives, that circumstance does not arise.

This call for continuous self-perfection might sound like a tall order—and it is. Changing ourselves is not easy but it is also not impossible. And, after all, why should it be easy? Excellence is not easy—good men are rare: "Good birth and virtue exist among few persons" (*Pol.* 1302a1). Even recognizing one's own limitations (much less doing something about them) can be difficult because knowing that one is not good enough requires some idea of what being good means. And, as just noted, poor upbringing can distort one's vision so that seeing one's limitations *as* limitations becomes impossible. Unless one recognizes the deficiencies in oneself change will not occur, because self-improvement is driven by that recognition, combined with a desire to be better than one is now. A person who does not recognize that there are problems with who and what she is will not attempt to change.

CONCLUSION

I began this project hoping that Aristotle would provide a grounding for ethics, answers which would persuade both Glaucon and Thrasymachus that they should be ethical. More precisely, I thought that he might show that we cannot be happy without being ethical. He would thereby establish that ethics provides genuine reasons for action by showing that it is necessary for the attainment of an end which we all pursue. Consequently, his argument should convince bad men and skeptics alike—as long as they are rational. We should be able to see now why Aristotle cannot provide such an argument. He does indeed believe that we cannot be truly happy without being ethical, and the *Ethics* presents an argument for the importance of ethical virtue in human life. However, that argument does not and cannot convince the bad person that true happiness requires virtue and that she therefore should be virtuous. Rejecting ethics, she can argue that virtue is unnecessary for (conative) happiness and that she is not interested in (normative) happiness.

Aristotle is well aware of this limitation and argues that arguments for and about ethics can be persuasive only to those who have been educated properly. The following passage, which I have quoted previously, expresses his view well:

> Arguments and teaching surely do not prevail on everyone, but the soul of the student needs to have been prepared by habits for enjoying and hating finely, like ground that is to nourish seed. For someone who lives in accord with his feelings would not even listen to an argument turning him away, or comprehend it [if he did listen]; and in that state

how could he be persuaded to change? And in general feelings seem to yield to force, not to argument. Hence we must already in some way have a character suitable for virtue, fond of what is fine and objecting to what is shameful. (1179b24–30)

As Williams notes, it is impossible to act and to develop rational arguments without accepting the principle of non-contradiction, but it is eminently possible to act and to argue while denying the importance of ethics.[1] Consequently, Socrates' intellectualism is misguided; bad people need not be irrational. They lack *phronêsis* but they are perfectly capable of figuring out how to reach their end. The problem is that they have chosen the wrong end, and they have done that because their desires are bad. Consequently, they do not need arguments, but rehabituation. They must learn to love the fine, coming to view the fine as providing reasons for action.

Ethics can be defended only by a joint appeal to reason and desire, and for those who lack the appropriate desires or have bracketed them the way the skeptic does, no argument will be persuasive. Therefore, I agree with Williams that we have to accept that ethical theories must start from inside ethics simply because there is nowhere else for them to start (1985, 93).[2] This means that the truth and value of ethics are apparent from the inside but cannot be conveyed to the outside. We can explain the role of ethics in a good life to those who already recognize that they should be ethical, reinforcing their belief that they are right to be ethical, and giving them some reasons for why that is so. However, we cannot explain it in a way that would persuade anybody who sincerely doubts either that ethics has a crucial role in a good life or that it provides independent reasons for action. Because he recognizes this, Aristotle addresses his argument to those who already believe that living well requires aiming at the fine.

We cannot answer Thrasymachus. How disturbing should that be? What are the consequences of the discovery that our ethical beliefs cannot be defended from the outside? What happens if we do not produce a grounding for ethics? Does that not mean that ethics will collapse now when nothing is holding it in place? Will we not be forced to accept that we have no good reason to be ethical? And then, are we not rationally compelled (even if emotionally reluctant) to go join Thrasymachus on the outside? A few years ago, a deeply religious fellow philosopher told me that he could not understand how I could be an ethical person, given my agnosticism. (I am pleased to report that my morals were not in question, merely their foundation.) Since I refused to ground my morality in God, where was I grounding it? My colleague viewed my ethical beliefs as hanging in the air and seemed worried that I would give them up once I finally recognized that nothing was holding them in place, once I read Dostoevsky and realized that without God, everything is permissible. At the time, I was unable to answer him to my own satisfaction, but I could not help thinking that my ethics seemed to be doing just fine without a foundation. It seems to me now that this last mentioned attitude is entirely appropriate. Williams puts the point well:

> It is a mistake . . . to think that there is some objective presumption in favor of the nonethical life, that ethical skepticism is the natural state, and that the person we have been imagining is what we all would want to be if there were no justification for the ethical life and we had discovered that there were none. The moral philosopher in search of justification sometimes pretends that this is so, overestimating in this respect the need for a justification just as he had overestimated its effect—its effect, at least, on the practicing skeptic. (1985, 26)[3]

We ought not let the bad man determine the terms of the debate. We should not accept that the default position is to stand outside of ethics or that skepticism and immorality are more natural to human beings than ethics. Consequently, it is mistaken to think that unless we find a strong foundation for ethics, the rational thing to do would be to abandon it. Once we reject these assumptions and mistakes, we need not accept that ethics must gracefully bow out if no proof of it is forthcoming. We must always remember that our inability to find an objective justification for ethics outside of ethics does not constitute a proof—or even a strong evidence—that ethics is a bad idea that should be abandoned. Thrasymachus does not reason badly—but neither do we. Indeed, an Aristotelian view of moral goodness and education implies that proof is not forthcoming because it indicates that proof would be impossible. Attempted proofs would either beg the question or defend ethics as an instrumental good and neither approach is acceptable. Recognizing the impossibility of such proof, we must stop thinking that we ought to suspend judgment until we are able to, in McDowell's words, put our Neurathian boat ashore "for a certification of its seaworthiness" (1995a, 216). There is no such shore, which means that Thrasymachus is on a ship too.

Neurath's sailor is a useful metaphor for explaining the ethical why. However, the comparison can be misleading. Perhaps most importantly, the sailor image suggests the possibility of more than one seaworthy vessel, but

Aristotle shows no signs of recognizing that there may be several different and good sets of ethical views. Because my focus has been on conversations with skeptics and bad people, I have not questioned the Aristotelian assumption that the ethical is one single system, in other words, that all good people hold largely the same views. But of course, this assumption is false. People from different cultures or historical periods disagree fundamentally about ethical issues, as do people from within the same culture. Indeed, we argue much more frequently with people who accept the importance of ethics but who disagree with us about its precepts than we do with Thrasymachus and his ilk. However, like our encounters with Thrasymachus, these confrontations often include jarring discoveries of deep disagreements. The other simply does not see things as I see them. One is, at first, tempted to assume that she will be convinced if she just listens to my argument. If she listens patiently and seems to understand but still shows no sign of changing her mind, it is tempting to adopt a new assumption: She must be either irrational or bad. Why else does she not understand what is so obvious? How can she not see that a fetus is a human being and thus should be afforded the same care and consideration as an infant? Or, from the other side of the abortion divide, how can she not see that decisions about a woman's body must be hers alone? Surely, if she were more rational, she would get it. But yet, assuming that she is irrational makes no sense. Her rationality shines forth; it is clear that she can argue and think quite well. The possibility that she is just bad remains and we often resort to it to explain our disagreement. And indeed, some of those who disagree with us may well be bad people. Others seem to be very good people, however; they are courageous, generous, and so on. In some cases, our only grounds for saying that those on the other side are not good is that they disagree with us about these thorny ethical issues. Surely, that is not enough. But if some or even many of the others are good and reasonable people, just as we are, why can we not reach a common understanding?

Our modified Aristotelian view explains these persistent disagreements by pointing out that many of our basic ethical convictions are acquired through habituation as well. While we can and do create arguments which justify them, we often do not hold such convictions because we have been persuaded by arguments, and when that is so, our convictions will not be altered by arguments. (I am not claiming that this is true about all our ethical views.) Rather, if such convictions change, they change either as a result of something akin to a conversion experience, or they change gradually over time, as we are rehabituated, reshaping ourselves or being reshaped into a new mold.

The situation is very similar to our conversations with Thrasymachus—we are arguing from different and perhaps incompatible starting points, which means that we will not be able to refute the other or prove the correctness of our views to their satisfaction. At best, both sides gain a deeper understanding about the nature of the disagreement by recognizing what their differences come down to, seeing that there are well-developed arguments for the other person's view, and then embarking upon a reexamination of their own views. Hopefully, in this dialogue, we will also find areas of agreement, leading us to recognize a second discrepancy between the sailor image and our ethical situation. The image suggests that different ethical systems are discrete and independent entities but, surely, they are overlapping.

This view of our ethical situation has important implications. First, it suggests that given our deep disagreements about ethics and the impossibility of rational agreement, we must allow more self-determination than Aristotle did and take a more negative attitude towards paternalism. The idea of self-determination is not foreign to Aristotle, who recognizes that making one's own choices is a crucial part of the good life. An agent who is not permitted to make his own decisions cannot live a good life. However, Aristotle subordinates self-determination to excellent virtuous activity. If self-determination promotes my virtuous activity, it is good; if it does not, it is bad, and should be curtailed. Thus, Aristotle does not consider rigid limits imposed upon people lacking virtue to be inherently problematic. In the ideal city, then, the citizens could and should be helped along through paternalistic measures whenever the rulers deem it necessary. Recognizing the limitations of arguments, we might, for instance, try to retrain those who we believe have misunderstood the ethical.

If our situation is as I have suggested, we simply cannot follow Aristotle here. Consider what acting paternalistically (rather than acting tyrannically) requires: I must know what is right and wrong better than others, and it must be possible for me to get them closer to their end against their will. My discussion should have cast some suspicion on whether either of these conditions can be fulfilled. We are much less confident about our ability to recognize the good than Aristotle was. Sometimes, we might feel certain that a particular action is virtuous and rational, but other times we hesitate, especially when we notice that others disagree with us.

Our lack of confidence in our vision of the good, combined with Aristotle's own insight that the good is not a simple or precise notion, should make contemporary Aristotelians much more hesitant about curtailing other people's self-determination than Aristotle was. We would be limiting their self-determination in order to direct them towards an end that we do not see clearly, along a path that we are not clear on, and when it is quite difficult to see if they in fact are approaching that end. In short, before we take it upon ourselves to improve them and their views, it behooves us to be very sure that we understand whether or not they are already engaging in excellent virtuous activity and how their activity can be improved.

To say that Aristotelian ethics needs to incorporate a greater emphasis on self-determination is to follow Nussbaum in suggesting that a contemporary Aristotelian ethics must be more Rawlsian. Rawls famously objects to Aristotelian ethics, arguing that Aristotle fails to recognize that the right must be prior to the good.[4] In a contemporary society, he argues, there will be a reasonable pluralism of views concerning the good, and self-determination requires that none of these will be imposed upon others:

> In a modern democratic society citizens affirm different, and indeed incommensurable and irreconcilable, though reasonable, comprehensive doctrines in the light of which they understand their conception of the good. . . . There is no politically practicable way to eliminate this diversity except by the oppressive use of state power. (2001, 84)

Thus, Rawls is trying to identify and argue for principles of justice that regulate the basic structure of a contemporary democratic society, while recognizing that such a society is too diverse and too big to be a genuine community. He is right, I think, to insist that on the macro level we must recognize reasonable pluralism. Contemporary democratic society is and will remain very diverse and we must coexist with people who fundamentally disagree with us. Thus, the views of the good that regulate our society must be minimal if they are going to have a chance to gain common support so that they can remain in effect without the use of oppressive force. However, we still need to decide how we try to improve ourselves and challenge those around us to greater virtue and thoughtfulness. And here, I think, an Aristotelian ethics can guide us. First, however, it must be tempered by the recognition that even when we feel completely certain that we are right, the fact that decent and thoughtful people disagree with us should make us less certain that we are right and they are wrong, and it should make us less eager to condemn them. We have to continually seek a balance between defending and questioning our views, even while arguing with people who see no need to reexamine their convictions, while yet hoping that we can persuade them to do so.

| *n o t e s*

Introduction

1. Needless to say, many philosophers have defended these ethical theories against such criticisms. I will not discuss this debate.

2. Anscombe writes: "It might remain to look for 'norms' in human virtues: just as *man* has so many teeth, which is certainly not the average number of teeth men have, but is the number of teeth for the species, so perhaps the species *man* regarded not just biologically, but from the point of view of the activity of thought and choice in regard to the various departments of life—powers and faculties and use of things needed—'has' such-and-such virtues: and this 'man' with the complete set of virtues is the 'norm', as 'man' with, e.g., a complete set of teeth is a norm" (1958, 40). For the purposes of my discussion, the important idea here is that we might be able to make human nature normative. I am not sure what to make of Anscombe's analogy between the development of virtues and the development of teeth. Acquiring virtue is a long and arduous process of habituation; teeth simply emerge. Furthermore, it is easy to be clear on what a complete set of teeth is, but much harder to determine what a complete set of virtues would be. The complete number of teeth does not vary depending on cultural practices; the complete number of virtues might.

3. Ross writes: "Aristotle's ethics is definitely teleological; morality for him consists in doing certain actions not because we see them to be right in themselves but because we see them to be such as will bring us nearer to the 'good for man.' This view, however, cannot really be reconciled with the distinction he draws between action or conduct, which is valuable in itself, and production, which derives its value from the 'work' . . . . If he had held fast to that distinction he would have reached a more Kantian type of theory. The distinction is not without influences on his ethics, but in the main category of means and ends is that by which he interprets human action" (1959, 184).

4. Copleston writes: "[According to Aristotle], there are natural tendencies implanted in man, the following of which in a general attitude of consistent harmony and proportion, i.e., recognizing relative importances and unimportances, is the ethical life of man. This view affords a basis for a natural as opposed to an arbitrary

ethics but considerable difficulties arise as to the theoretical establishment of moral *obligation*" (1946, 333).

5. Williams also argues that Aristotle is trying to "elicit the good for man out of man's nature"; and he seems to think that Aristotle is trying to "elicit unquestionable moral ends or ideals from distinguishing marks of man's nature" and to "found morality on a conception of the *good man* elicited from considerations of the distinguishing marks of human nature" (1976, 56–59, 61).

6. Irwin writes: "Knowledge of a human being as essentially a rational agent is the basis of an account of the human good and of responsible rational agency from which the rest of the account of the virtues is derived. When we understand the place of rational agency in the human essence, we can describe the complete good and identify its dominant component" (1988, 468).

7. Annas stresses that she leaves open whether the grounding facts about nature are evaluative or ethical (1993, 137), and Nussbaum writes that the conception of a human being from which the argument starts is itself normative: "The conception of the human being is itself, in a certain way, a normative conception, in that it involves singling out certain functions as more basic than others" (1992, 227).

8. "According to this [other] view, Aristotle thinks that we should *first* define what a human being is, and *then*, on the basis of that definition, we will know what the human good is. My thesis is that we discover what we are only after we have run through all of the arguments concerning what our ultimate end should be" (Kraut 1989, 353n.34).

9. "According to virtue theorists, one is supposed to use the concept of flourishing to develop an account and justification of the virtues. Flourishing is the prior notion and the virtues are to be understood in terms of it. But Aristotle's understanding of the relation between flourishing and the virtues is the opposite of this . . . . So the notion of virtue must be prior to the notion of *eudaimonia* and must be understood before *eudaimonia* can be understood" (P. Simpson 1992, 507). In Simpson's view, Aristotle's point is not that we should be virtuous because it will lead to *eudaimonia* but rather that we should accept his understanding of *eudaimonia* because it gives a prominent place to the virtues.

10. "It is often thought that this Aristotelian realism points to an extra-ethical basis for reflection about what *eudaimonia* consists in. The idea is that, in Aristotle's view, it is possible to certify that a virtuous person's conception of *eudaimonia* is genuinely correct . . . . I do not believe there is any sign of this supposed external validation in Aristotle's text. On the contrary, trying to read it into him disrupts our understanding of things he actually says" (McDowell 1995a, 202–3).

11. Hereafter, the *Nicomachean Ethics* is referred to as the *Ethics*. References from the *Ethics* will be given by the standard page and line numbers, without the title. Unless otherwise noted, I quote Irwin's translation (Aristotle 1999). Citations from any other works will be prefaced by title. Quotes from the *Politics* use Lord's translation unless otherwise noted (Aristotle 1984c).

12. I suspect that Plato recognized that such conversations would not change bad men and that the conversations with bad men in the Platonic dialogues are actually not for the benefit of the bad men at all but rather for the sake of the other interlocu-

tors and listeners. If Plato had been more optimistic about the impact of Socrates' argument on men like Thrasymachus, surely he would have depicted Thrasymachus as being persuaded by Socrates.

Chapter one. **Being and Becoming Good**

1. Aristotle argues that decision is "most proper to virtue" and that the way we make decisions "distinguish[es] characters from one another better than actions do" (1111b5).

2. I say "generally" because in my view Aristotle makes allowances for the fact that we in some situations do not have time for deliberation before we choose and act. Some critics have complained that by requiring deliberation to precede action, Aristotle makes it impossible to act rightly in situations where we lack time for deliberation. Situations that require courage, for example, might require us to act before thinking—if we pause to think, it might be too late, and needing to think might seem to be a sign of a moral failing. This complaint seems to ignore the following passage: "If we are warned in advance, we might decide what to do [not only because of our state of character, but] also by reason and rational calculation; but in emergencies [we must decide] in accord with our state of character" (1117a20–25). Aristotle's acknowledgment that we sometimes can and should decide without first deliberating is important because it suggests that he recognized that one can decide without deliberating, basing the decision upon deliberation that was done before in similar cases and on the existing shape of one's character.

3. This is not reason's only task. Reason is also crucially involved in figuring out whether the end should be pursued at all.

4. Finally, it is possible to live poorly through incontinence (*akrasia*). This might seem to be the same as desiring bad ends, but it is a bit different. The incontinent person acts against decision and reason: "Incontinence is against one's decision" (1151a6). The incontinent person seems to be the same as one who "abandons . . . [his rational calculation, and acts] because of his feelings" (1145b13–14). They act "not, however, because they have decided on it, but against their decision and thought [*tên prohairesin kai tên dianoian*]" (1148a9).

5. "Fine" and "noble" seem to be the most common choices in the contemporary literature. Irwin, Sherman and Annas use "fine"; McDowell and Miller list both but generally use "noble"; Burnyeat, Apostle and Korsgaard use "noble."

6. Owens is well aware of these difficulties, but he believes they can be overcome if we stick to the ordinary language sense of "right" expressed in "this is the right thing to do."

7. "Beautiful" is too purely aesthetic; "moral goodness" imports "morality" which in my view has too many non-Aristotelian connotations (especially Kantian ones); "noble" and "honorable" do not hint at the aesthetic dimension of *kalon*.

8. See also the following passages: "Brave people act because of the fine [*dia to kalon*], and their spirit cooperates with them" (1116b30–31); "He will endure them because that is fine [*hoti kalon*] or because failure is shameful" (1117b9); "The

magnificent person will aim at the fine [*tou kalou heneka*], for that is a common feature of the virtues . . . [and] he will think more about the finest and most fitting way
to spend than about the cost" (1122b5–10); "[The vulgar person] aims not at the fine
[*ou tou kalou heneka*] but at the display of his wealth" (1123a25); "We praise the
honor-lover for being manly and a lover of the fine [*philokalon*]" (1125b13); "[The
friendly person] will aim to avoid causing pain or to share pleasure, but will always
refer to the fine and the beneficial" (1126b29).

    9. I am in accord with Sorabji on this point: "The man who chooses to do the
virtuous act for its own sake may choose it not because it is required by some particular virtue, such as courage, but because it is required by virtue in general. Thus
Aristotle often speaks as if this man thinks in rather general terms of what is required
by *to kalon* (the noble). But it makes little difference either way, for the man who
thinks more specifically in terms of what is required by virtue. This will become
clearer later when we discuss the unity of the virtues. We shall then see that considerations of what courage requires involve considerations of what the other virtues
require" (1974, 203).

    10. Cf. Irwin (1999, 195, §7).

    11. McDowell writes: "In acquiring the virtues of character, a person is taught to
admire and delight in actions as exemplifying the value of nobility. Coming to value
the noble integrally includes an alteration in one's motivational make-up, in what one
finds attractive: it shapes one's conception of what is worth going in for" (1995a, 209).

    12. A failure of reason is of course possible too; I might desire to do the fine but
be unsure about what means I need to select.

    13. I borrow this list of passages from Owens, who writes: "In fact, the Greek
term *kalon* and the impersonal *dei* ('it ought' or 'it should') are used interchangeably
in the *Ethics*. The one carries the same meaning as the other" (1981, 30).

    14. Annas writes: "Aristotle recognizes that the virtuous person does the virtuous
action for its own sake, and, further, that when she so acts she is motivated in a dis-
tinctive way" (1993, 123, see also 75). "'For the sake of the fine' is functioning rather
like the Kantian notion of doing one's duty for the sake of doing one's duty; it char-
acterizes what morality requires" (ibid., 370). Similarly, Christine Korsgaard writes:
"As for nobility [*kalon*], Aristotle seems to think of it very much as Kant thinks of
good will—it is the specific kind of *intrinsic* value that moral actions and those who
possess them possess" (1996, 216–17; see her footnotes for some qualifications).

    15. I am relying upon Williams' distinction between ethics and morality here. As
Williams defines the terms, morality is a narrower notion, a particular kind of ethics,
which focuses upon the concept of obligation, regarding it as the only kind of truly
moral consideration. He views Kant as its primary spokesperson. Ethics, on the other
hand, recognizes several kinds of ethical consideration, including not only obligation
but also action and virtue. (See Williams 1985, especially chapter 10).

    16. Sherman writes: "Aristotle's distinction between the fine and the advanta-
geous . . . will bear some resemblance to the distinction between the moral and
the non-moral; to act for the sake of the fine is, as we have said, to value as eminently worthwhile the exercise of the virtues directed at the common good . . . .
But there is no clear sense in Aristotle of a specific class of considerations having

preemptive status over others" (1989, 122). Nussbaum writes: "I shall, in fact, try to avoid not only the Kantian moral/non-moral distinction, but all versions of that distinction and of the related distinctions between moral and non-moral practical reasoning, moral and non-moral practical conflict. The Greek texts make no such distinction. They begin from the general question, 'How should we live?' and consider the claim of all human values to be constituent parts of the good life; they do not assume that there is any one group that has even a *prima facie* claim to be supreme" (1986, 5n).

17. This, incidentally, is why "noble" is a good choice as a translation.

18. Even when he is speaking about the person with *megalopsychia*, a person who is difficult to recognize as ethical, he is still talking about what we should be like.

19. Cf. Burnyeat: "The word love is not idly used; Aristotle has in mind a disposition of the feelings comparable in intensity, though not of course in every other respect, to the passion of a man who is crazy about horses" (1980, 76).

20. It also occurs in 10.9 where Aristotle speaks about "a well-born character that truly loves what is fine [*philokalon*]" and a character that is "fond of what is fine [*stergon to kalon*]" (1179b9, 1179b30) and in 4.4 where he writes that "we praise the honor-lover for being manly and a lover of the fine [*philokalon*]" (1125b13).

21. Something very similar happens in Advaita Vedanta. I attain liberation when I come to know that I am Brahman but of course saying it and believing what I say is not enough. I must experience it as true.

22. This is of course only part of his definition. It continues: "consisting in a mean, the mean relative to us, which is defined by reference to reason, that is to say, to the reason by reference to which the prudent person would define it" (1107a1–3). I will not discuss Aristotle's doctrine of the mean but rather focus upon his claim that virtue that is a *hexis prohairetikê*, a state that decides how to act and which does so well.

23. Cf. Irwin (1999, 349, entry on "state").

24. This, incidentally, is why Irwin argues that "disposition" and "habit" are bad translations of *hexis*; *hexis* involves one's feelings and desires as well as one's decisions (1999, 349, entry on "state").

25. See for example Grant (1885, 482–83, 486, 241–42) and Stewart (1892, 171). Sherman, of course, criticizes the mechanical view (see 1989, especially 157–99), as do Burnyeat (1980) and Sorabji (1974). My own understanding of Aristotelian habituation is strongly influenced by Sherman's argument.

26. I find Sorabji's explanation of this very plausible: "Aristotle ascribes a major role to the intellect . . . . But it needs to be acknowledged that he does something else. He tends to present the various parts of his view in isolation and to concentrate on each part in turn to such an extent as to give us the wrong impression of what the whole view will be. The emphasis on habit at the beginning of Book 2 is only one of many cases" (1974, 218).

27. See also 1095a2–4, 1095b2–8, *Pol.* 1336b6.

28. I am speaking here of full virtue. Natural virtue certainly can exist without *phronêsis*, as can the various forms of incomplete or inferior virtues, like the virtue of a slave or a woman (see *Politics* and cf. Sorabji 1974, 213–14).

29. Now, as McDowell notes, this distinction between knowing that and knowing why is not as clear cut as it seems because it seems impossible to know that I should do something but have no response to the question of why I should do it (1995a, 215), even if my answer is only "because my father says so," "because it is an action that is honorable," or "because it is fine."

30. McDowell notes that Aristotle "registers at least the possibility of graduating from having only the *that* to having the *because* as well. He leaves room for a transition to a comprehending acceptance of a scheme of values" (1995a, 212). My position is that ethical goodness, for Aristotle, requires that transition to comprehension.

Chapter two. **The Kantian Challenge**

1. Wood writes: "To [Kant] Aristotle was, apart from being the proponent of the false doctrine that virtue was a mean between two vices, one of the many eudaimonists of antiquity whose views were to be rejected" (1996, 141). In addition, Kant refers to Aristotle as "chief of the *empiricists*" (CPR B882).

2. I will not raise the issue about whether this dilemma is appropriately attributed to David Hume.

3. This paragraph and those that follow have benefited greatly from Caswell's discussion of the issue (2002).

4. See for instance Allison 1990, 110.

5. Korsgaard labels it a "double aspect theory of motivation" (1996, 208).

6. This seems to be a very questionable assumption. Can we not also be motivated by love and benevolence; must those motivations really be reduced to self-interest? In places, Kant seems to agree. For example, he writes that "it is a very beautiful thing to do good to men because of love and a sympathetic good will, or to do justice because of a love of order" (CPrR 5:83). Here, those motivations seem to be different from self-interest.

7. I am indebted to Korsgaard for drawing my attention to this passage.

8. Cf. Korsgaard 1996, 213.

9. My thinking on this issue is indebted to Korsgaard but even more to Sherman (1989). Korsgaard argues that it is a disagreement about "what inclination is which in turn depends on a difference in their views of what pleasure and pain are" (1996, 223). I would suggest that the underlying disagreement is more about their view of inclinations and the possibility of reforming inclinations (and thus about human nature).

10. In the *Critique of Practical Reason*, Kant uses this "fact of reason" to prove that we are free: We stand under the moral law; we can stand under the moral law if and only if we are free; therefore, we must be free. The problem with such an argument, of course, is that it seems to ignore the possibility that we are deluded about standing under the moral law. In the *Groundwork*, his argument goes in the other direction, arguing that if we are free, we stand under the moral law.

11. See also *EE* 1221b20.

Chapter three. **The Unethical Theoretician**

1. My position on this issue is quite similar to and to some extent indebted to that of Richard Kraut (1989).

2. Here, I agree with Cooper (1975, 99–100) and Kraut (1989).

3. Scholars favoring an inclusivist interpretation of *eudaimonia* believe that "the best and most complete virtue" refers to an inclusive one—that is, all of the virtues together. Sherman writes: "I am not persuaded by the view that there are already foreshadowings of this position in the statement of the formal criteria of happiness in NE 1.7. For this to be the case, we would have to read *teleiotatên* in 1.7 ('most final or most complete') as implying an exclusive end, singled out above all others. . . . I see no reason for this exclusionary interpretation" (1989, 95n48).

4. But contrast this with Aristotle's comment about Thales in the *Politics*, where he describes Thales as making money through his skill in reading the stars (1259a5–18).

5. Cf. Wilkes: "The indecision in Aristotle's ethics arises directly from the bilateral nature of Aristotle's man [being animal and divine] and cannot be evaded" (1978, 352).

6. My view is, I think, essentially the same as to that of Kraut and of Sherman.

7. Nussbaum rejects the divine ideal as a model for human beings on Aristotle's behalf: "The life of a divine being might be ever so admirable; but the study of this life, insofar as it lies beyond our capabilities, is not pertinent to the practical aim of ethics" (1986, 293). Thus, Nussbaum insists, Aristotle's theology does not affect his ethics. I do not think this is right. However, it is crucial to understand what Aristotle means by saying that we should imitate God.

8. Inferior beings participate as they are able in vital activities that model the divine, and thus become divine to the extent they can: "Reproduction and the use of food; for it is the most natural function in living things, such as are perfect and not mutilated or do not have spontaneous generation, to produce another thing like themselves—an animal to produce an animal, a plant a plant—in order that they may partake of the everlasting and divine in so far as they can; for all desire that, and for the sake of that they do whatever they do in accordance with nature. . . . Since, then, they cannot share in the everlasting and divine by continuous existence, because no perishable thing can persist numerically one and the same, they share in them in so far as each can, some more and some less; and what persists is not the thing itself but something like itself, not one in number but one in species" (*De Anima* 415a22–b8, Hamlyn translation).

9. Cf. Amelie Rorty: "While objects that do not change at all are paradigmatic cases of what is contemplated, it is also possible to contemplate the unchanging form of what does change. Species meet that requirement" (1980a, 379).

10. It still seems to me, however, that if the point is to know God, studying God directly rather than through his effects in the world would be more effective. But perhaps human beings can know God only through studying how he affects the world?

11. Irwin translates the passage "study seems to be liked because of itself alone," thus avoiding the difficulty. It does not seem to me that the Greek can be translated

in that way, or, at least, that it would be the natural way of translating the passage in question (cf. Kraut, 1989, 190 n.15). *Monê* seems clearly grammatically connected to *autê*, not to *di' hautên*.

12. On this point, I agree with Kraut (1989).

13. Notice that this complicates the value of the ethical virtues. They are not valuable per se but merely valuable given the human condition. As Nussbaum writes, "their nature *and* their goodness are constituted by the fragile nature of human life" (1986, 341). For human beings, however, Aristotle argues that they are valuable in themselves; they are not merely instrumentally valuable.

14. See also the *Ethics* 1.2: "Even if the good is the same for a city as for an individual, still the good of the city is apparently a greater and more complete good to acquire and preserve. For while it is satisfactory to acquire and preserve the good even for an individual, it is finer and more divine to acquire and preserve it for a people and for cities" (1094b8–11).

15. This needs qualifications, of course, or we make Aristotle sound too much like Kant. Certain people have claims upon us, fellow citizens and immediate family being the primary examples, whereas others, like the slaves of other people, do not.

16. Kraut directed my attention to this passage (1989, 97–103).

17. Cf. Kraut: "These fellow citizens are owed a certain way of being treated, *whether or not treating them in that way maximizes your interest*" (1989, 101).

18. It seems to me that Sherman is interpreting Aristotle correctly on this point, and I think it is the most sensible view. It is less clear to me, however, that he *should* believe this, logically speaking. If contemplation is so superior, exactly why does it fail to have preemptive status?

19. Thus, I would tend to agree with Williams: "What Aristotle does not do, however—and granted his system, cannot do—is to provide any account of how the intellectual activities, the highest expression (in his view) of man's nature, are to be brought into relation to the citizenly activities which are regulated by the virtues of character . . . [I]t is a curious, and significant, feature of Aristotle's system that the highest potentialities of man have admittedly to compete with others for expression, but no coherent account can be given of how this is to be regulated" (1976, 56).

Chapter four. **The Argument of the *Ethics*: Discerning and Reaching the Highest End**

1. "*Pasa technê kai pasa methodos, homoiôs de praxis te kai prohairesis, agathou tinos ephiesthai dokei: dio kalôs apethênanto tagathon, hou pant' ephietai*" (1094a3).

2. However, I do not think that Aristotle's ethics needs a teleological view of the universe as a whole. A teleological account of rational action seems to be sufficient.

3. See my discussion of decision making in chapter 1.

4. I am borrowing the conative/normative distinction from Irwin. I follow him in lossing a conative conception of the good as one upon which "one's good will be relative to one's desires and aims" and a normative conception as one where "the

complete good is determined by objective norms and standards, beyond the agent's desires" (1988, 362–63).

5. Aristotle says that he will examine the life of study later. Presumably, then, when he says at the end of the chapter, "Let us, then, dismiss [these candidates]" (1096a10), he does not mean to dismiss *theôria*; it has yet to be discussed.

6. What is said to be lower than happiness is virtue, not virtuous activity, understanding, not the activity of understanding.

7. Irwin argues that Aristotle reaches the conclusion that there is only one highest end by assuming that "a rational agent can pursue only one such end" (1988, 361). This line of reasoning strikes me as problematic. It is true that it would be preferable if we only had one highest end because that would reduce and perhaps even eliminate the possibility of conflicts between different goals and priorities, hence making rational action easier. But the fact that it is preferable does not make it true.

8. I am indebted to Richard Kraut (1979) for drawing my attention to this issue and to the passage from the *Topics*.

9. Here I disagree with, among others, Irwin and Wilkes, who suggest that the function argument relies upon *De Anima* (Irwin, 1988, 363; Wilkes, 1978, 343). I agree, of course, that Aristotle is using the terminology of *DA* here, but I do not believe that the argument requires it.

10. We are also the only animal that has managed to separate reproduction and sexuality, but that too seems to be an ability that is contingent upon our rational activity.

11. See Kraut (1989).

12. I am indebted to Whiting (1988, 37) for directing my attention to this passage.

13. Cf. Whiting (1988, 35–36); Fred Miller: "In speaking of the function as *idion*, [Aristotle] does not mean that it is 'peculiar' or 'unique' to human beings but, instead, that it is 'proper,' in the sense of 'essential,' to human beings" (1995, 348); and Thomas Nagel, who notes that reason is "what human life is all about," while all other functions are for its sake (1972, 11).

14. Cf. Wilkes: "If the dog could run, bark, and see without eating, it would still be a *dog* (however unusual), whereas if it could only take in nourishment, it would be an oddly shaped vegetable" (1978, 345).

15. Recall the distinction that Aristotle draws in 1.1 between ends that are products apart from the activity and ends that are activities. In the case of boat building, the end is a boat, a product resulting from the performance of an *ergon* that is entirely separate from the boat. In the case of the eye, however, seeing is both the *ergon* and the *telos*.

16. I mean "skill" in the loosest sense possible, simply to mean "being good at doing something." I do not mean to imply that virtuous living is a *technê*, especially not one that can be formalized in a series of steps.

17. Cf. Korsgaard (1986, 260).

18. Compare to the discussion of what code of behavior might be entailed by the existence of a highest end earlier in the chapter. Korsgaard's discussion of the instrumental role of virtue is very helpful (1986, esp. 277), but she does not note that this establishes only an instrumental use.

19. I take that to be McDowell's point in the following passage: "What Aristotle achieves by invoking the *ergon* of a human being is only this: he enables himself to represent his thesis that the good *for man* is activity in accordance with human virtue as a specific case of a general connection between good and virtue, or excellence. What he exploits is a conceptual link between an X's being such as to act as it befits an X to act and its having the excellence that is proper to an X. The conceptual link is truistic, and it leaves entirely open what sort of evaluative or normative background fixes a substance for applications of the notions of *ergon* and excellence, in any particular exemplification of the general connection" (1995a, 208).

Chapter five. **Answering Those Who Do Not Love the Fine**

1. John McDowell first drew my attention to this point (1995a and 1995b). He suggests that Aristotle is not trying to ground anything and that this thesis is suggested by Aristotle's choice of audience. McDowell further argues that the assumptions that virtue needs an external foundation and that practical reason must be validated based on natural facts are modern assumptions that Aristotle did not make. Once we start looking for such a foundation, we think that perhaps the relevant facts are those about what animals like us need, and then we attribute our assumptions to Aristotle.

2. This distinction is spelled out in the same way by, among others, Irwin (1999, 339, entry on "nature"), Annas (1993) and McDowell (1995b, see especially 170).

3. Cf. MacIntyre: "We thus have a threefold scheme in which human-nature-as-it-happens-to-be (human nature in its untutored state) is initially discrepant and discordant with the precepts of ethics and needs to be transformed by the instruction of practical reason and experience into human-nature-as-it-could-be-if-it-realized-its-*telos*" (1984, 53).

4. See the introduction for some examples.

5. See for example Cooper (1975, 82), Ackrill (1978), and Irwin (1999, 205, §9, note on *ta pros to telos*). Cooper puts the point very well: "Although [Aristotle] does hold that virtuous action is a means to *eudaimonia*, or human good, *eudaimonia* is itself not specified independently of virtuous action; on the contrary, *eudaimonia* is conceived of as identical with a lifetime of morally virtuous action (together perhaps with other activities as well)" (1975, 88). MacIntyre argues in a similar vein: "What constitutes the good for man is a complete human life lived at its best, and the exercise of the virtues is a necessary and central part of such a life, not a mere preparatory exercise to secure such a life . . . . And within an Aristotelian framework the suggestion therefore that there might be some means to achieve the good for man without the exercise of the virtues makes no sense" (1984, 149).

6. "Happiness is a certain sort of activity of the soul in accord with complete virtue" (1102a5); "The happy life is one in accordance with virtue and unimpeded" (*Pol.* 1295a34); "Happiness is the best thing, and this is the actualization of virtue and a certain complete practice of it" (*Pol.* 1328a37–38); "Happiness is the actualization

and complete practice of virtue, and this not on the basis of a presupposition but unqualifiedly" (*Pol.* 1332a9–10).

7. Here, I agree with Irwin (1999, 243, §6).

8. See n. 1 in this chapter.

9. Cf. Annas: "How one's feelings and emotions have developed affects the way one can now achieve a grasp of what the right thing to do is. . . . Arguments are important in ethics, but on their own, they do not make people virtuous; changes in ethical belief have to become rooted in one's emotional life before they become effective" (1993, 54).

10. Burnyeat writes: "In Aristotle's view it is no good arguing or discussing with someone who lacks the appropriate starting points ("the *that*") and has no conception of just or noble actions as worthwhile in themselves, regardless of contingent rewards and punishments. To such a person you can recommend the virtues only insofar as they are required in a social order for avoiding the pain of punishment—that is, for essentially external, contingent reasons. You cannot guarantee to be able to show that they will contribute to some personal goal the agent already has, be it power, money, pleasure, or whatever; and even if in given contingent circumstances this connection with some antecedent personal goal could be made, you would not have given the person reason to pursue the virtues for their own sake, as a *part* of happiness, but only as a means to it" (1980, 81).

11. "Thought by itself moves nothing: what moves us is goal-directed thought concerned with action [and] . . . acting well is the goal and desire for the goal. That is why decision is either understanding combined with desire or desire combined with thought, and this is the sort of principle that a human being is" (1139b1–5).

12. For an interesting discussion of protreptic arguments, see Whiting (2001, 95–98). I am not persuaded that this is a helpful way of reading Irwin's interpretation of Aristotle, however.

13. On this point, I am agreeing with Burnyeat (1980, 81) against McDowell (1995a, 213).

14. Here, I agree with Burnyeat, who writes: "If [Aristotle] is setting out 'the *because*' of virtuous actions [in the *Ethics*], he is explaining what makes them noble, just, courageous, and so on, and how they fit into a scheme of the good life, not why they should be pursued at all. He is addressing someone who already wants and enjoys virtuous action and needs to see this aspect of his life in a deeper perspective. He is not attempting the task too many moralists have undertaken of recommending virtue even to those who despise it . . . . Rather, he is giving a course in practical thinking to enable someone who already wants to be virtuous to understand better what he should do and why. Such understanding, as Aristotle conceives it, is more than merely cognitive" (1980, 81).

15. See for instance 1094b23–25, 1095a10, and 1103b30.

16. Aristotle suggests that "the intemperate person is incurable" (1150b32).

17. In Aristotle's view, I think, the unity of virtue holds only for the person who has perfect *phronêsis*. Somebody who has perfect courage must also have *phronêsis* and therefore must also have all the other virtues: "[It is argued that] since the same person is not naturally best suited for all the virtues, someone will already have one

virtue before he gets another. This is indeed possible in the case of the natural virtues. It is not possible, however, in the case of the [full] virtues that someone must have to be called good without qualification; for one has all the virtues if and only if one has *phronêsis*" (1144b34–45a2). For those of us who are not good without qualification, it is quite possible to be, for instance, rather courageous without also being temperate. The *Rhetoric* makes this clear (see 1390b).

Conclusion

1. Cf. Williams: "Ethical skepticism of this sort differs so much from skepticism about the external world that it cannot be treated by the same methods. Moore famously disconcerted the skeptic about material objects by confronting him with one, Moore's hand . . . . There has been much discussion about the effect of Moore's gesture . . . but it undoubtedly has some effect, in reminding us that to take such a skeptic seriously might be to take him literally, and that there is some problem about what counts as doing that. There is no analogy here to the ethical. It may possibly be that if there are any ethical truths, some of them can be displayed as certain . . . but the production of such an example does not have the same disquieting effect on the ethical skeptic as the display of Moore's hand on the other kind" (1985, 24–25).

2. Williams writes: "Ethical theories have to start from somewhere. Earlier I considered ways of their starting outside ethics altogether. I also touched upon the idea of starting inside ethics, but merely from the meaning of moral words. I found all of these in varying degrees unpersuasive . . . . [We] still have to start from somewhere, and the only starting point left is ethical experience itself" (1985, 93).

3. However, Williams does not agree with my reading of Aristotle seeming instead to think that Aristotle is trying to ground ethics. His interpretation is forcefully criticized by John McDowell (1995b).

4. In *A Theory of Justice* (1971), Rawls suggested that the main disagreement between himself and Aristotle is about the priority of the right to the good, and he argued that we must determine what is right independently of what is good. In Rawls's theoretical "original position," in which the social contract is drawn up behind a "veil of ignorance," the participants decide on principles of justice without knowledge of their specific conceptions of the good, and with no advance knowledge of how they themselves will fare in the actual society. Rawls has modified his view on this point. In *Justice as Fairness*, he agrees with his critics that it is impossible to determine what is just without recourse to a notion of what is good. However, he still argues that the right must be prior to the good (2001, 140).

works cited

Ackrill, J. L. 1978. "Aristotle on *Eudaimonia*." *Mind* 87:595–601. (Rpt. in Rorty 1980b, 15–33.)

Allison, Henry. 1990. *Kant's Theory of Freedom*. Cambridge: Cambridge University Press.

Annas, Julia. 1993. *The Morality of Happiness*. New York: Oxford University Press.

Anscombe, G. E. M. 1958. "Modern Moral Philosophy." *Philosophy* 31:1–19. (Page refs. are to rpt. in Crisp and Slote 1997, 26–44.)

Anton, J. P. and A. Preus, eds. 1991. *Essays in Ancient Greek Philosophy: Aristotle's "Ethics."* Albany: State University of New York Press.

Aristotle. 1890. *Ethica Nicomachea*. Ed. I. Bywater. Oxford: Oxford University Press, 1970.

———. 1926. *Rhetoric*. Trans. J. H. Freese. Cambridge, Mass.: Harvard University Press.

———. 1932. *Politics*. Trans. H. Rackham. Cambridge, Mass.: Harvard University Press, 1990.

———. 1935a. *Eudemian Ethics*. Trans. H. Rackham. Cambridge, Mass.: Harvard University Press, 1996.

———. 1935b. *On The Soul*. Trans. W. S. Hett. Cambridge, Mass.: Harvard University Press, 1995.

———. 1979. *Metaphysics*. Trans. Hippocrates G. Apostle. Grinnell, Iowa: Peripatetic Press.

———. 1983. *De Anima. Books II and III with Passages from Book I*. Trans. D. W. Hamlyn. Oxford: Clarendon Press.

———. 1984a. *Nicomachean Ethics*. Trans. Hippocrates G. Apostle. Grinnell, Iowa: Peripatetic Press.

———. 1984b. *Physics*. Trans. R. P. Hardie and R. K. Gaye. In *The Complete Works of Aristotle*. Ed. Jonathan Barnes. Princeton: Princeton University Press.

———. 1984c. *Politics*. Trans. Carnes Lord. Chicago: Chicago University Press.

———. 1999. *Nicomachean Ethics*. Trans. Terence Irwin. 2nd ed. Indianapolis: Hackett.

Augustine. 1961. *Confessions.* Trans. R. S. Pine-Coffin. London: Penguin.

Burnyeat, M. F. 1980. "Aristotle on Learning to Be Good." In Rorty 1980b, 69–92.

Caswell, Matt. 2002. *Kant and the Highest Good.* Ph.D. diss. Boston University.

Cooper, John M. 1975. *Reason and Human Good in Aristotle.* Cambridge, Mass.: Harvard University Press.

———. 1987. "Contemplation and Happiness: A Reconsideration." *Synthese* 72: 187–216.

Copleston, Frederick C. 1946. *A History of Philosophy.* Vol. 1, *Greece and Rome.* New York: Doubleday, 1993.

Crisp, Roger, and Michael Slote, eds. 1997. *Virtue Ethics.* Oxford: Oxford University Press.

Engstrom, Stephen. 1996. "Happiness and the Highest Good in Aristotle and Kant." In Engstrom and Whiting 1996, 102–140.

Engstrom, Stephen, and Jennifer Whiting, eds. 1996. *Aristotle, Kant and the Stoics.* Cambridge: Cambridge University Press.

Grant, A. 1885. *The Ethics of Aristotle.* London: Longmans, Green.

Heinaman, Robert, ed. 1995. *Aristotle and Moral Realism.* Boulder, Colo.: Westview Press.

Holmes, Stephen Taylor. 1979. "Aristippus In and Out of Athens." *American Political Science Review* 73:113–28.

Irwin, T. H. 1980. "The Metaphysical and Psychological Basis of Aristotle's *Ethics.*" In Rorty 1980b, 35–54.

———. 1988. *Aristotle's First Principles.* Oxford: Oxford University Press.

———. 1996. "Kant's Criticism of Eudaimonism." In Engstrom and Whiting 1996, 63–101.

———. 1999. Trans. intro. to *Nicomachean Ethics.* 2nd edition. Indianapolis: Hackett.

Kant, Immanuel. 1956. *Critique of Practical Reason.* Trans. Lewis White Beck. New York: Macmillan.

———. 1960. *Religion within the Boundaries of Mere Reason.* Trans. Allen Wood and George DiGiovanni. Cambridge: Cambridge University Press.

———. 1965. *Critique of Pure Reason.* Trans. Norman Kemp Smith. New York: St. Martin's Press.

———. 1981. *Grounding for the Metaphysics of Morals.* Trans. J. Ellington, 1981. Indianapolis: Hackett.

———. 1996. *Metaphysics of Morals.* Trans. M. Gregor. Cambridge: Cambridge University Press.

Korsgaard, Christine. 1986. "Aristotle on Function and Virtue." *History of Philosophy Quarterly* 3:259–79.

———. 1996. "From Duty and for the Sake of the Noble: Kant and Aristotle on Morally Good Action." In Engstrom and Whiting 1996, 203–36.

———. 1998. "Kant's Analysis of Obligation: The Argument of *Groundwork I.*" In *Kant's "Groundwork of the Metaphysics of Morals": Critical Essays,* ed. Paul Guyer, 51–80. New York: Rowman & Littlefield.

Kraut, Richard. 1979. "The Peculiar Function of Human Beings." *Canadian Journal of Philosophy* 9:467–78.

———. 1989. *Aristotle on the Human Good*. Princeton, N.J.: Princeton University Press.

Lewis, C. S. 1960. *The Screwtape Letters*. New York: Macmillan.

MacIntyre, Alasdair. 1966. *A Short History of Ethics*. New York: Macmillan.

———. 1984. *After Virtue*. 2nd ed. Notre Dame, Ind.: Notre Dame University Press.

McDowell, John. 1980. "The Role of *Eudaimonia* in Aristotle's *Ethics*." *Proceedings of African Classical Associations* 15:1–15. (Page refs. are to rpt. in Rorty 1980b, 359–76.)

———. 1995a. "Eudaimonism and Realism in Aristotle's *Ethics*." In Heinaman 1995, 201–18.

———. 1995b. "Two Sorts of Naturalism." In *Virtues and Reasons: Philippa Foot and Moral Theory*, ed. R. Hursthouse, G. Lawrence, and W. Quinn, 149–79. Oxford: Clarendon Press.

Miller, Fred D. 1995. *Nature, Justice, and Rights in Aristotle's Politics*. Oxford: Clarendon Press.

Montague, Phillip. 1992. "Virtue Ethics: A Qualified Success Story." *American Philosophical Quarterly* 29:53–61.

Nagel, Thomas. 1972. "Aristotle on *Eudaimonia*." *Phronêsis* 17:252–59. (Page refs. are to rpt. in Rorty 1980b, 15–34.)

———. 1986. "Review of Bernard Williams' *Ethics and the Limits of Philosophy*." *Journal of Philosophy* 83:351–60.

Nozick, Robert. 1981. *Philosophical Explanations*. Cambridge, Mass.: Harvard University Press.

Nussbaum, Martha. 1986. *The Fragility of Goodness: Luck and Ethics in Greek Tragedy and Philosophy*. Cambridge: Cambridge University Press.

———. 1992. "Human Functioning and Social Justice: In Defense of Aristotelian Essentialism." *Political Theory* 20:202–46.

Owens, Joseph. 1981. "The *Kalon* in the Aristotelian *Ethics*." In *Studies in Aristotle*, ed. D. J. O'Meara, 261–77. Washington, D.C.: Catholic University Press.

Rawls, John. 1971. *A Theory of Justice*. Cambridge, Mass.: Belknap Press of Harvard University Press.

———. 2001. *Justice as Fairness: A Restatement*. Ed. Erin Kelly. Cambridge, Mass.: Belknap Press of Harvard University Press.

Rorty, Amelie. 1980a. "The Place of Contemplation in Aristotle's *Ethics*." In Rorty 1980b, 377–94.

———, ed. 1980b. *Essays on Aristotle's Ethics*. Berkeley: University of California Press.

Ross, W. D. 1959. *Aristotle: A Complete Exposition of His Work and Thought*. New York: New American Library, Meridian Books.

Sherman, Nancy. 1989. *The Fabric of Character: Aristotle's Theory of Virtue*. Oxford: Clarendon Press.

Simpson, Peter. 1992. "Contemporary Virtue Ethics and Aristotle." *Review of Metaphysics* 45:503–24.

Simpson, R. W. 1975. "Happiness." *American Philosophical Quarterly* 12:169–76.

Sorabji, Richard. 1974. "Aristotle on the Role of Intellect in Virtue." *Proceedings of the Aristotelian Society* n.s. 74:107–29. (Page refs. are to rpt. in Rorty 1980b, 201–20.)

Stewart, J. A. 1892. *Notes on the Nicomachean Ethics of Aristotle, i and ii.* New York: Arno Press, 1973.

Sullivan, R. J. 1989. *Immanuel Kant's Moral Theory.* New York: Cambridge University Press.

———. 1994. *An Introduction to Kant's Ethics.* Cambridge: Cambridge University Press.

Whiting, Jennifer E. 1988. "Aristotle's Function Argument: A Defense." *Ancient Philosophy* 8:33–48.

———. 2001. "Strong Dialectic, Neurathian Reflection, and the Ascent of Desire: Irwin and McDowell on Aristotle's Methods of Ethics." *Proceedings of the Boston Area Colloquium in Ancient Philosophy*, vol. 17, ed. John J. Cleary and Gary M. Gurtler, S.J., 61–116. Leiden and Boston: Brill.

Wilkes, Kathleen V. 1978. "The Good Man and the Good for Man in Aristotle's *Ethics.*" *Mind* 87:553–71. (Page refs. are to rpt. in Rorty 1980b, 341–58.)

Williams, Bernard. 1976. *Morality: An Introduction to Ethics.* Cambridge: Cambridge University Press.

———. "Philosophy." 1981. *The Legacy of Greece: A New Appraisal.* Ed. M. I. Finley. Oxford: Clarendon. 202–55.

———. 1985. *Ethics and the Limits of Philosophy.* Cambridge: Harvard University Press.

Wood, Allen W. "Self-Love, Self-Benevolence, and Self-Conceit." In Engstrom and Whiting 1996, 141–61.

index

Ackrill, J. L., 130n.5
Advaita Vedanta, 61, 125n.21
Allison, Henry, 30–31, 36, 126n.4
Anaxagoras, 53
Annas, Julia, 123n.5, 130n.2
  on arguments for ethics, 131n.9
  on Book 10, 52–53
  on happiness and virtue, 101
  on human nature, 4, 122n.7
  on *kalon*, 15–16, 124n.14
  on virtues of thought vs. virtues of
    character, 52–53, 59
Anscombe, G. E. M.
  on human nature, 121n.2
  "Modern Moral Philosophy," 2–3
Apostle, Hippocrates, 123n.5
arguments for ethics, 1–4, 5, 10, 71–95,
  131n.9
  and desire, 26, 47, 93–95, 98, 107–9,
    110, 115–16
  and habituation, 103–5, 118–19
  from happiness (*eudaimonia*), 6–7,
    68–69, 97, 99–102, 104, 115
  from human function, 6, 50, 53,
    68–69, 71, 72, 73, 81–95, 97,
    129n.9
  from human nature, 3–4, 6–7, 66,
    67, 97, 98–102, 104, 121nn.2, 4,
    122n.5, 130n.3
  moral improvement through, 109–14

and Neurath's sailor, 105, 117–18
  See also foundations for ethics
Augustine, St., 56

bad persons, 5, 10, 18, 71, 97–98, 112
  desire in, 26, 47, 68, 93–95, 98,
    107–9, 110, 115–16
  as intemperate, 68, 99, 111, 131n.16
  Plato's Thrasymachus, 1–2, 3, 4, 7,
    28, 108–9, 110, 115, 116, 117, 118,
    119, 122n.12
  as rational, 3, 26, 68, 83, 92, 107–8,
    115, 116, 117
  theoreticians as, 67–69, 72, 94, 95, 100
Burnyeat, M. F., 123n.5, 125n.25, 131n.13
  on knowing why vs. knowing that,
    24–25
  on loving the fine, 125n.19
  on objects of choice, 13
  on virtue, 17–18, 131nn.10, 14

Caswell, Matt, 126n.3
categorical imperatives, 5–6, 45–46, 68
continence, 14, 15, 17–18, 20, 28, 34, 37,
  101, 110
Cooper, John M., 127n.2
  Reason and Human Good in Aristotle,
    59
  on *theôria* and ethics, 59
  on virtue and happiness, 130n.5

ANNA LÄNNSTRÖM

is assistant professor of philosophy at Stonehill College.